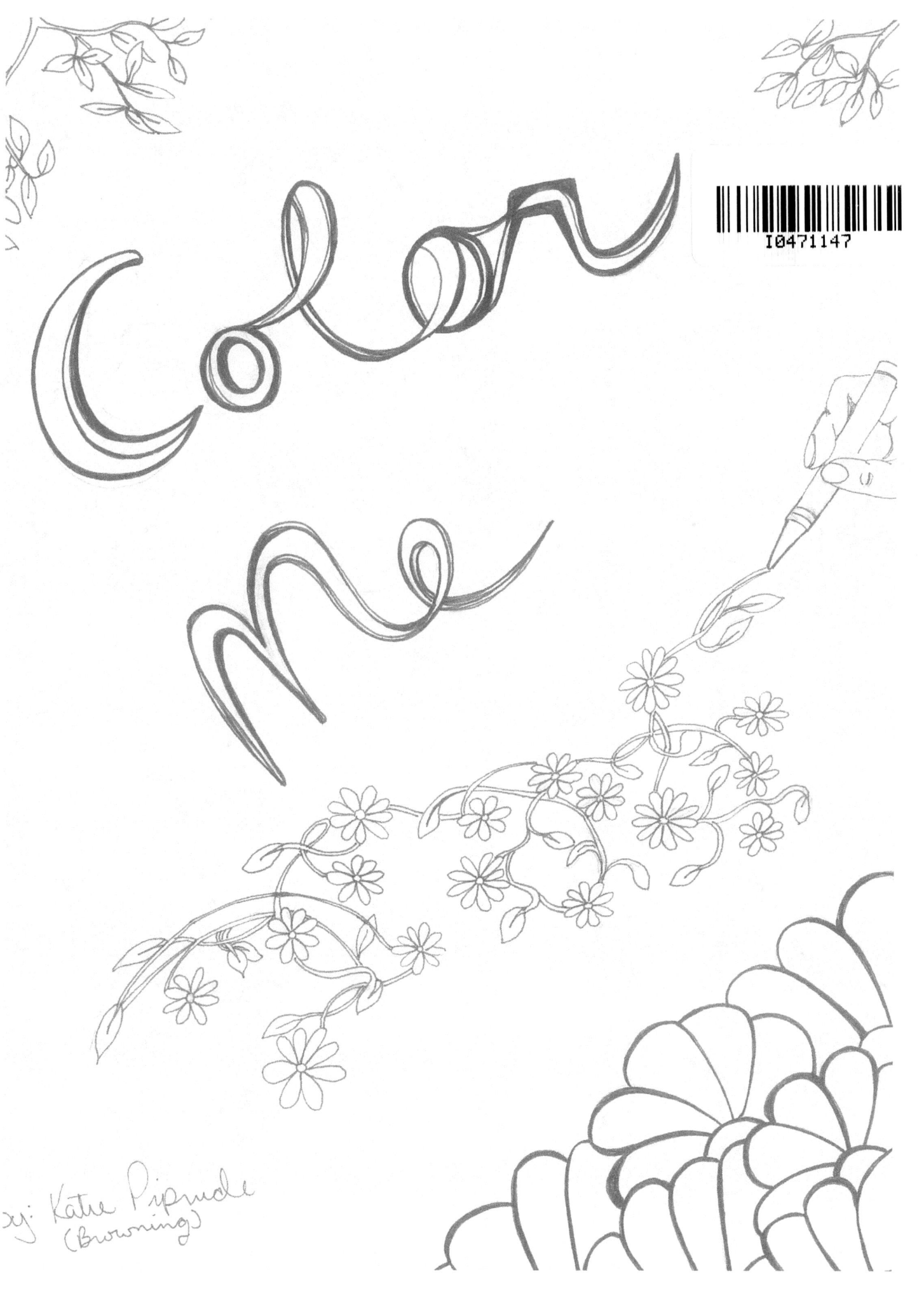

Color me

xj: Katie Pipmole
(Browning)

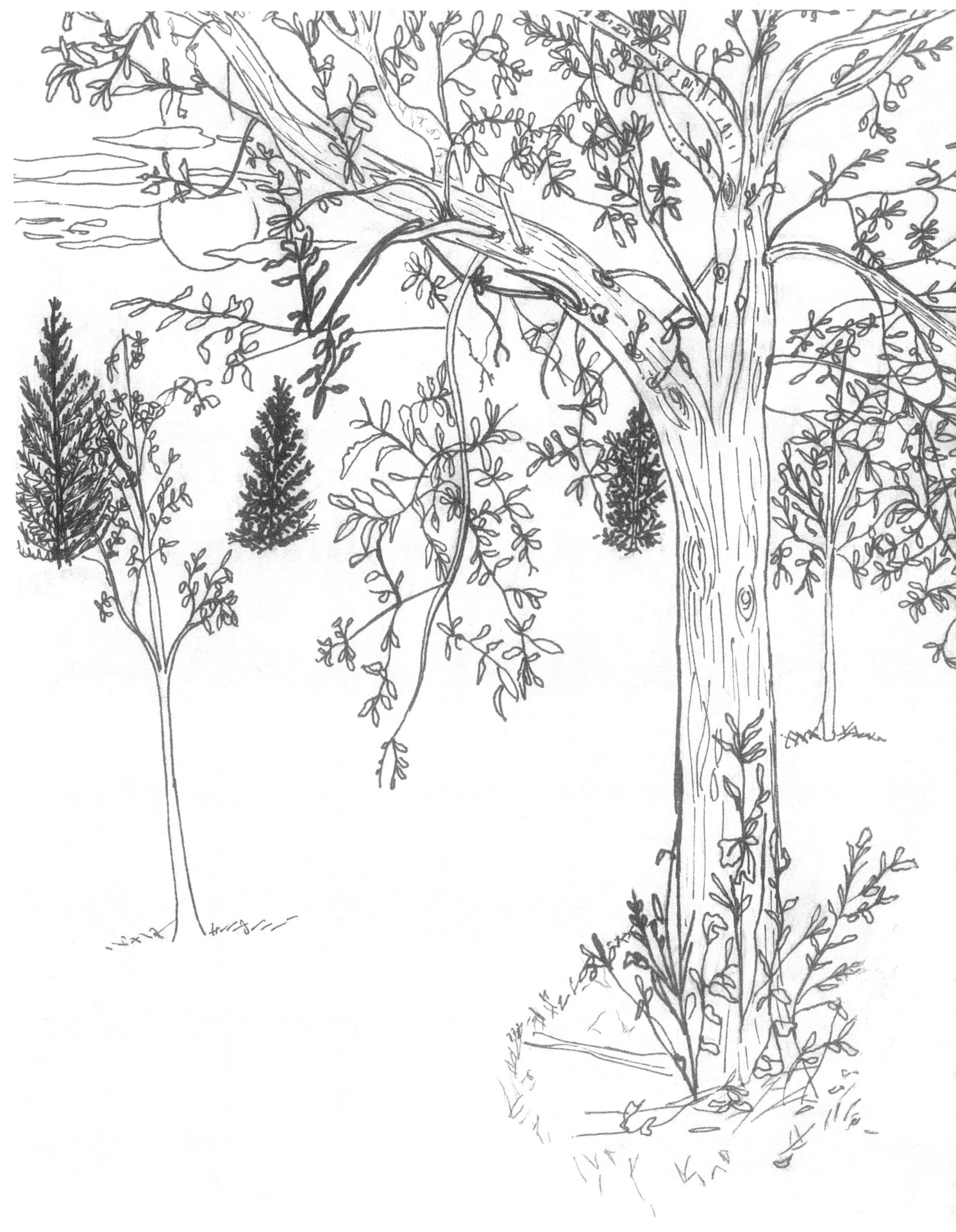

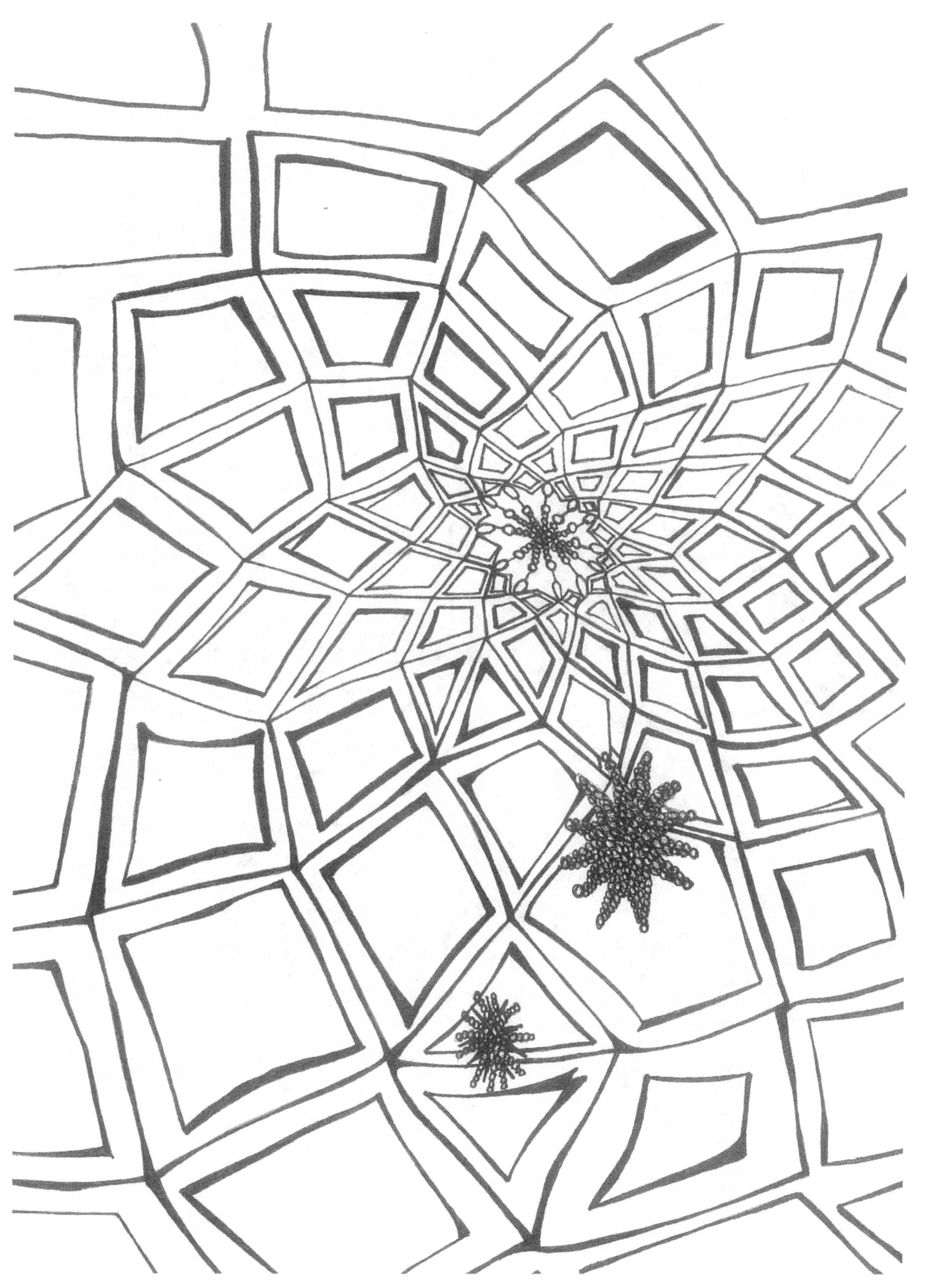

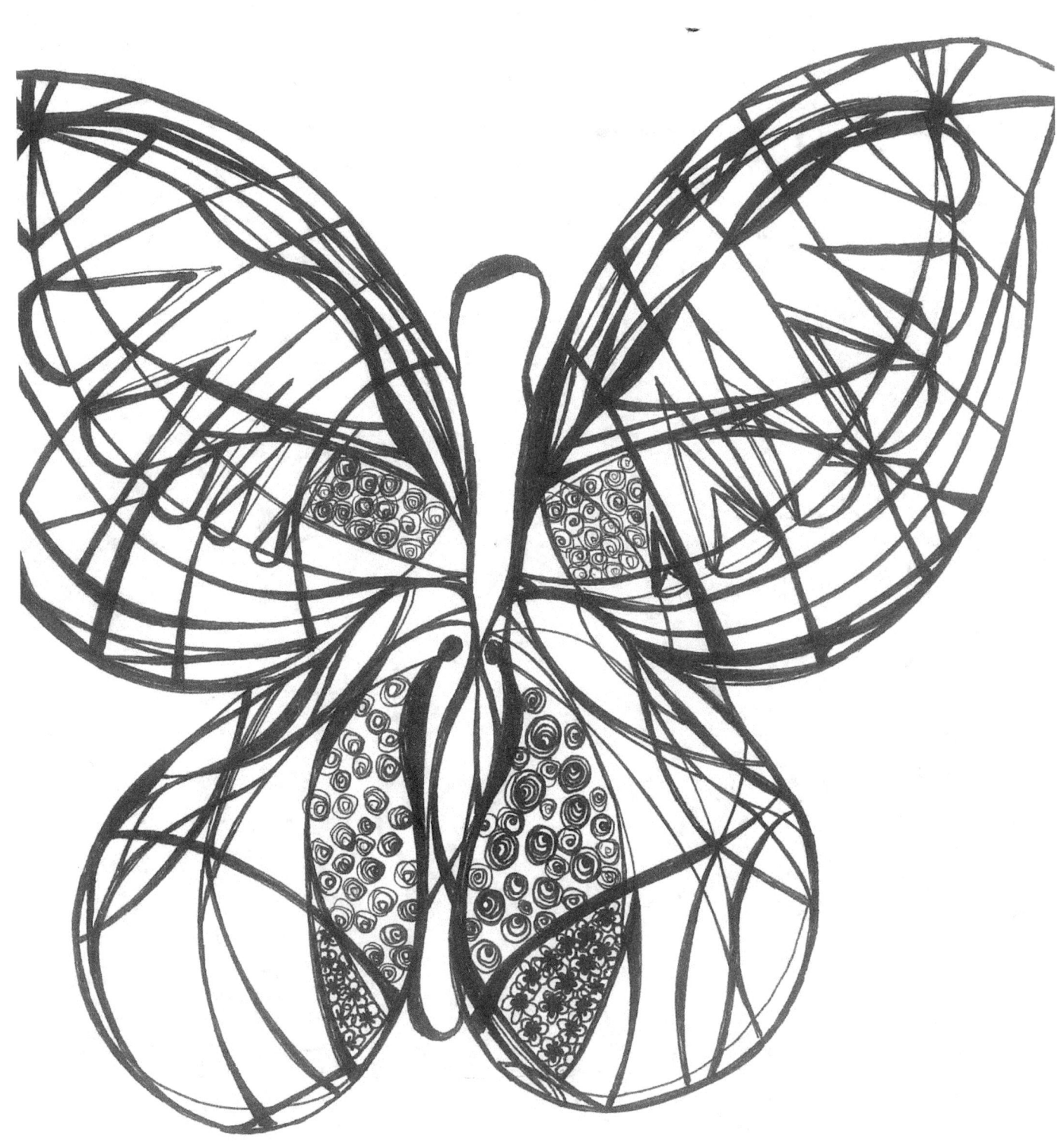

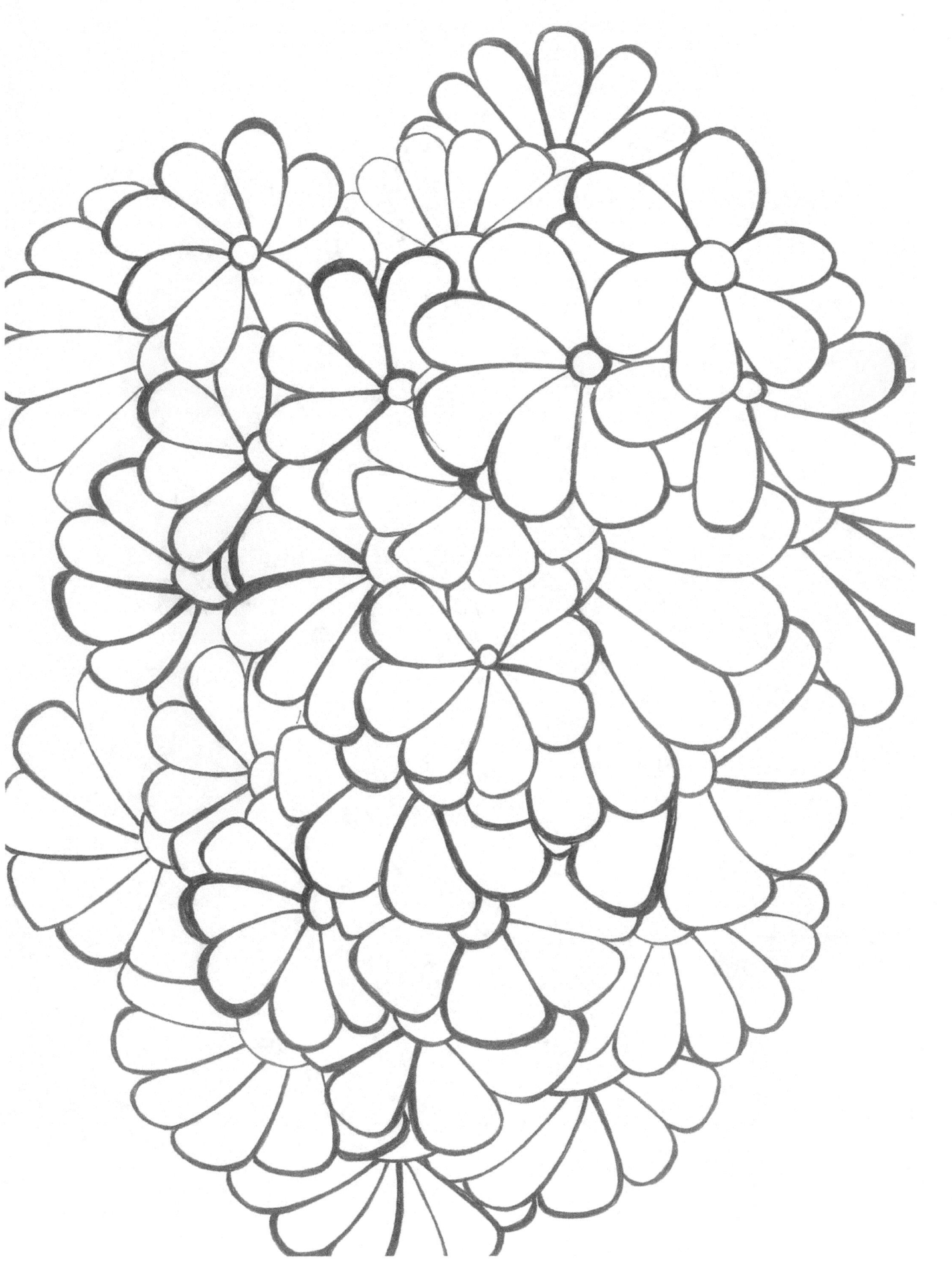

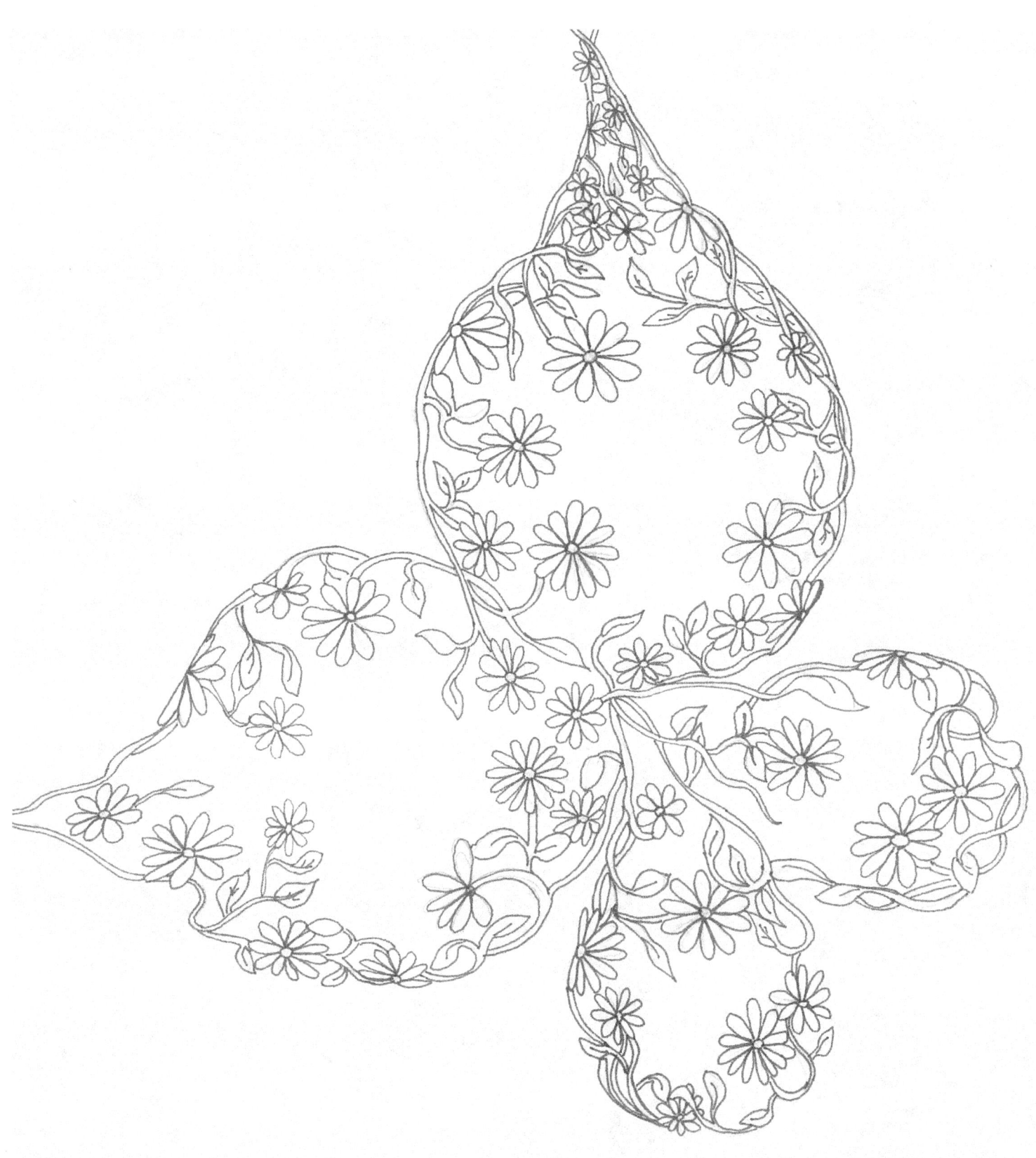

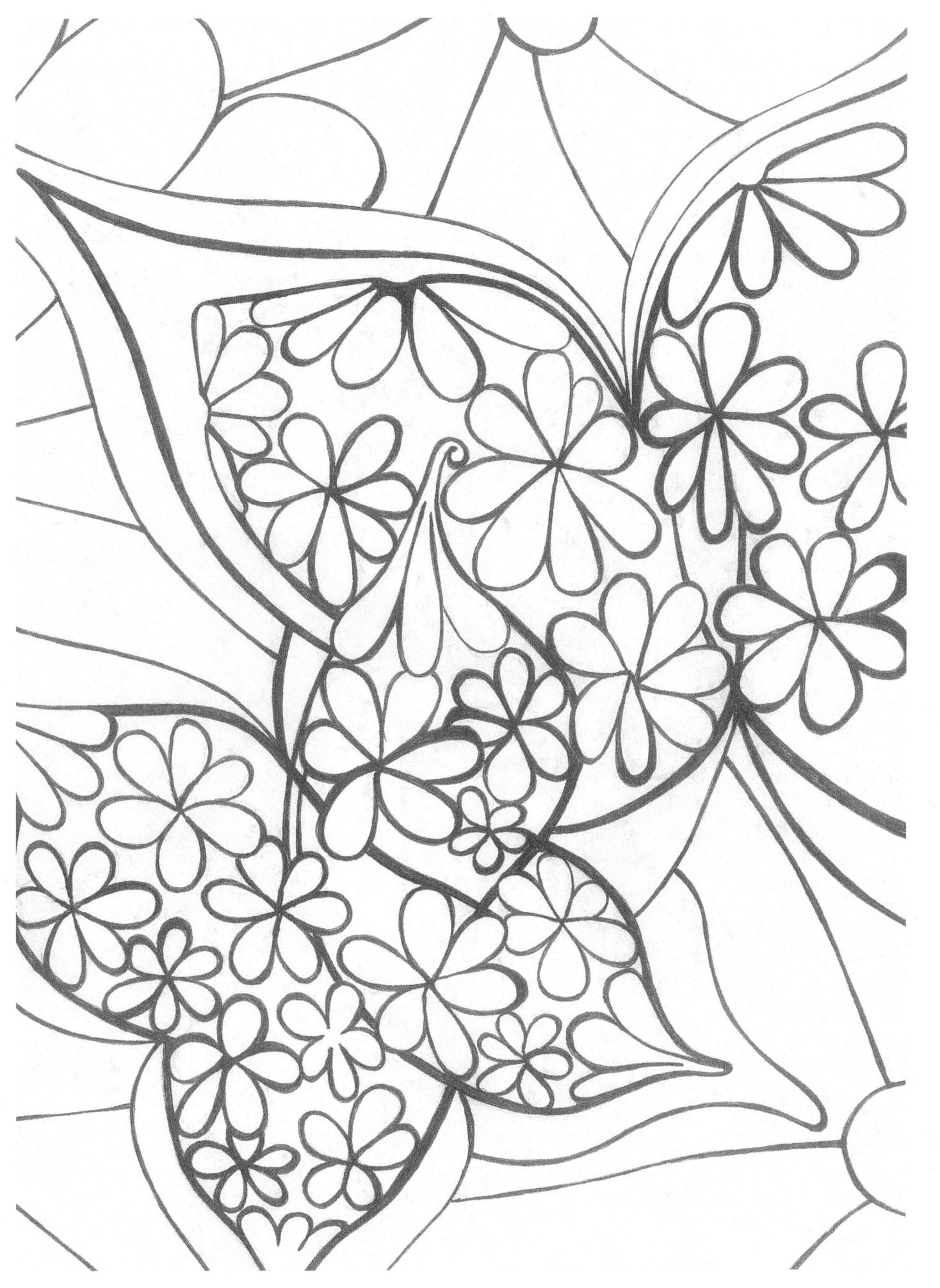

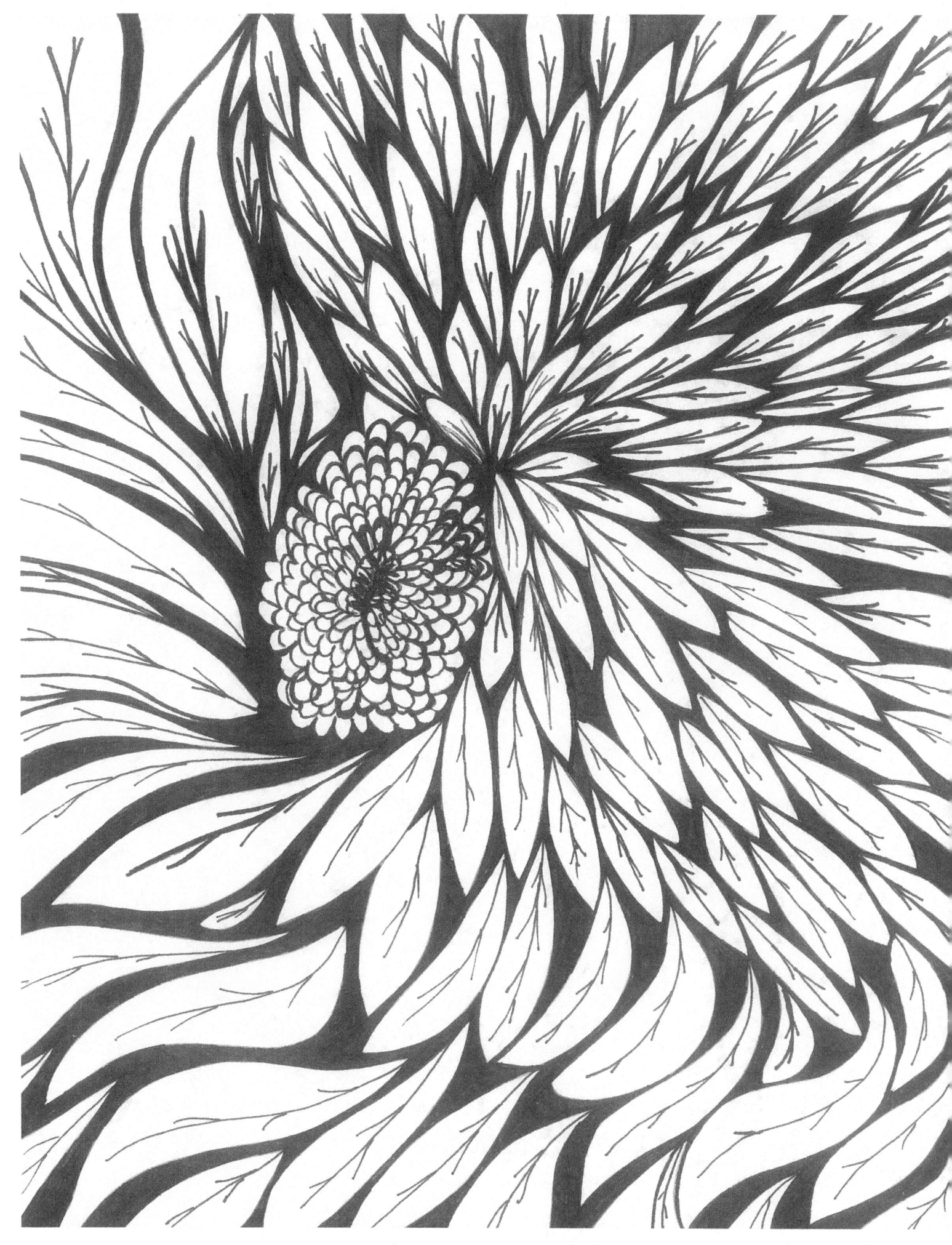

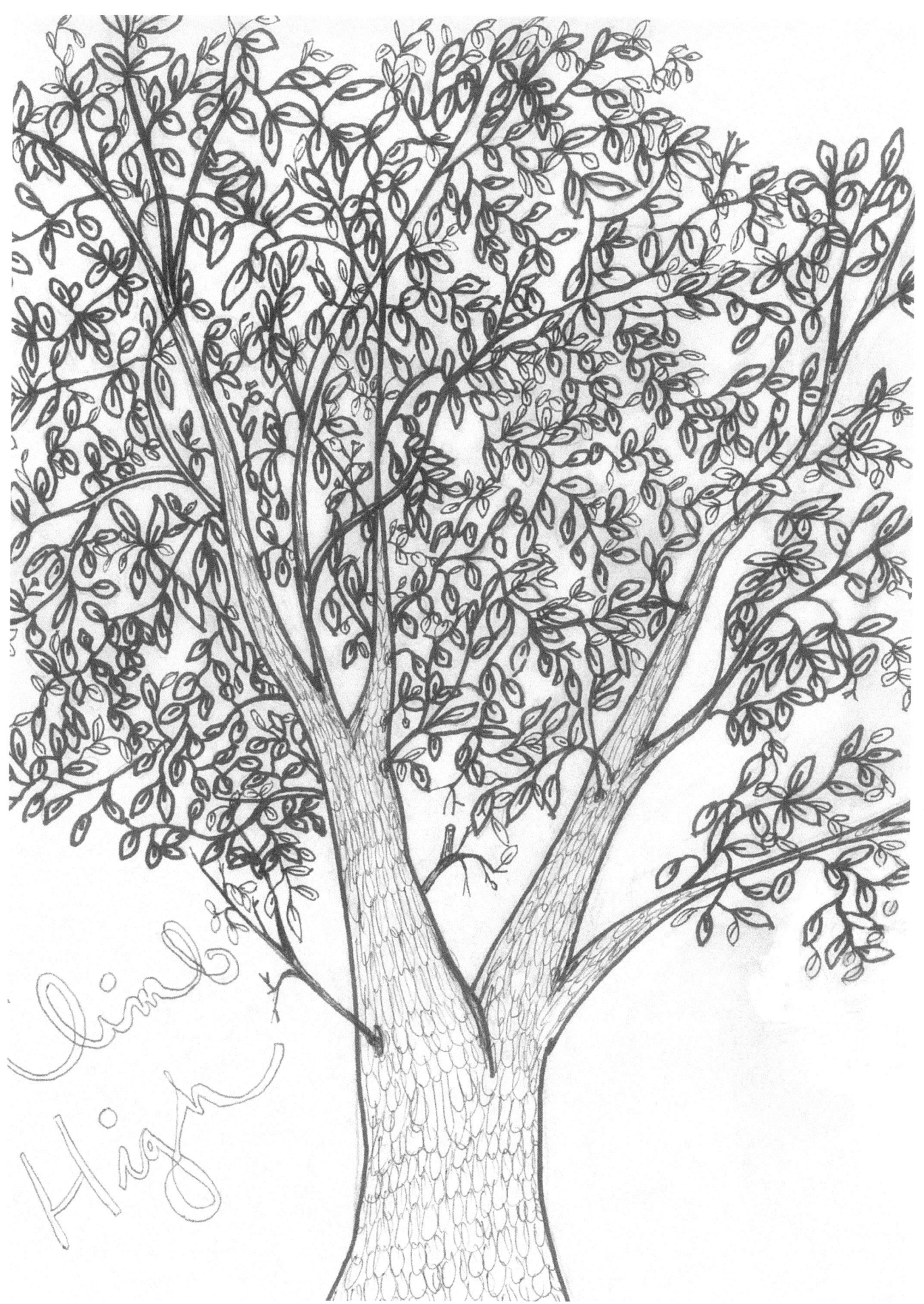

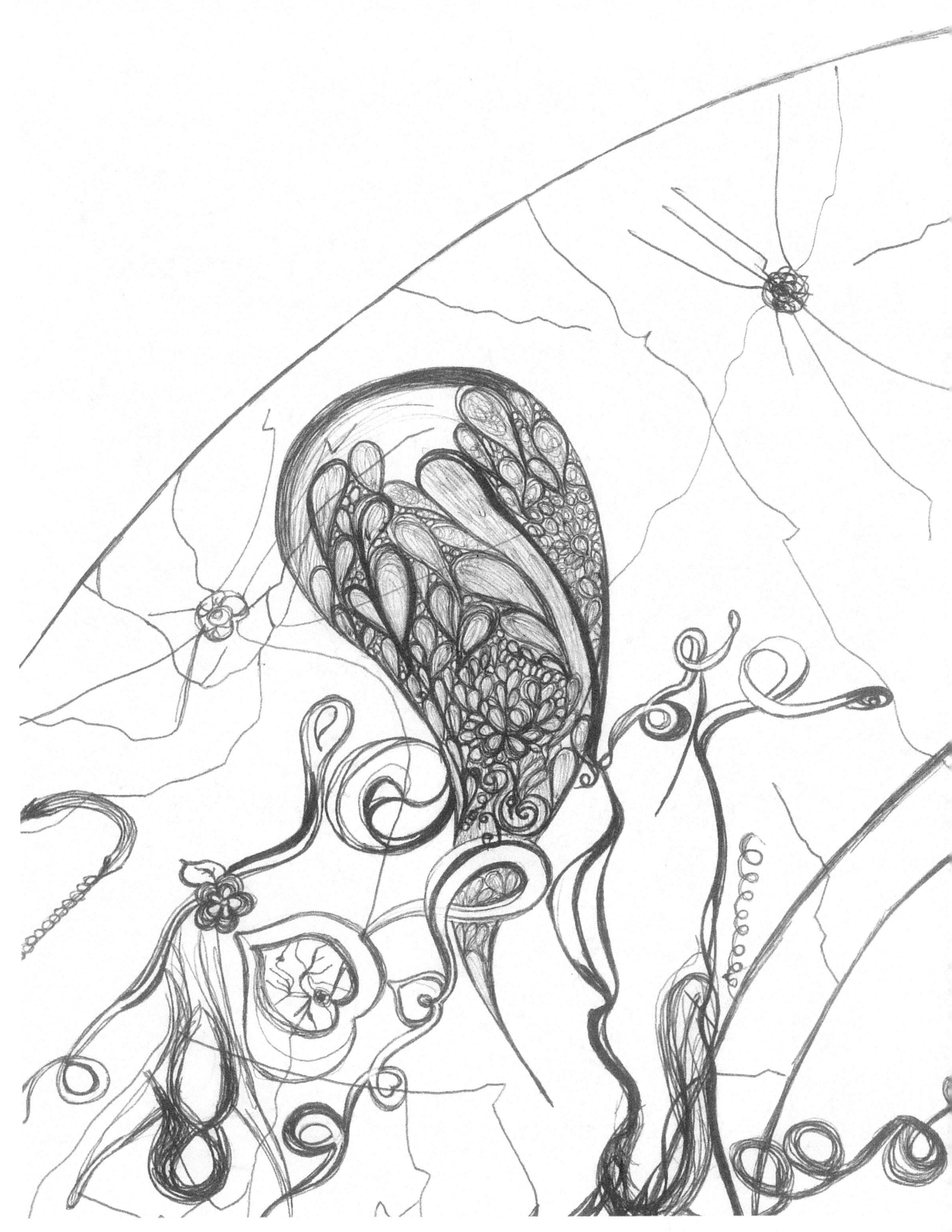

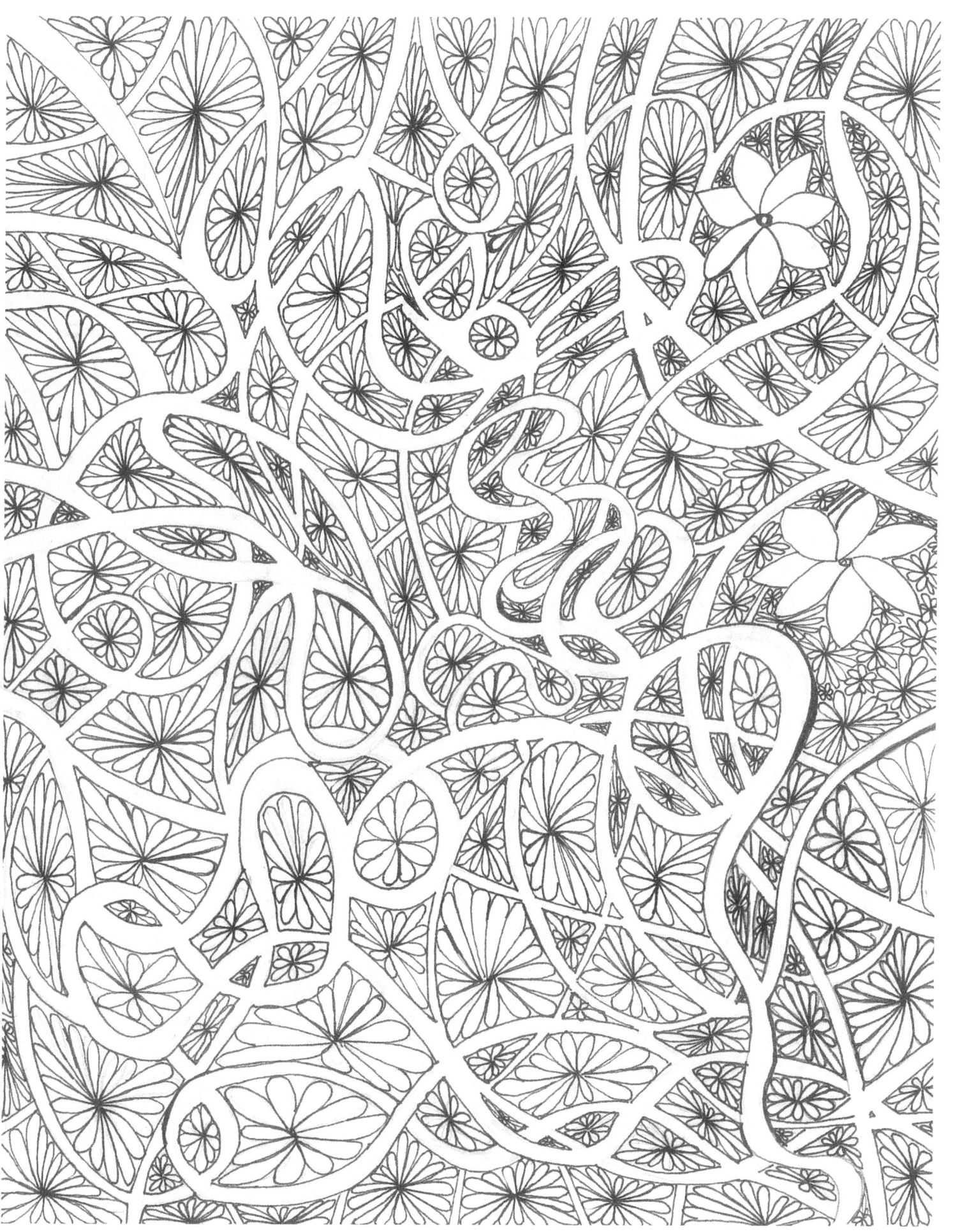

Its not what you do for your children but what you teach them to do for themselves that makes them sucessful human beings.

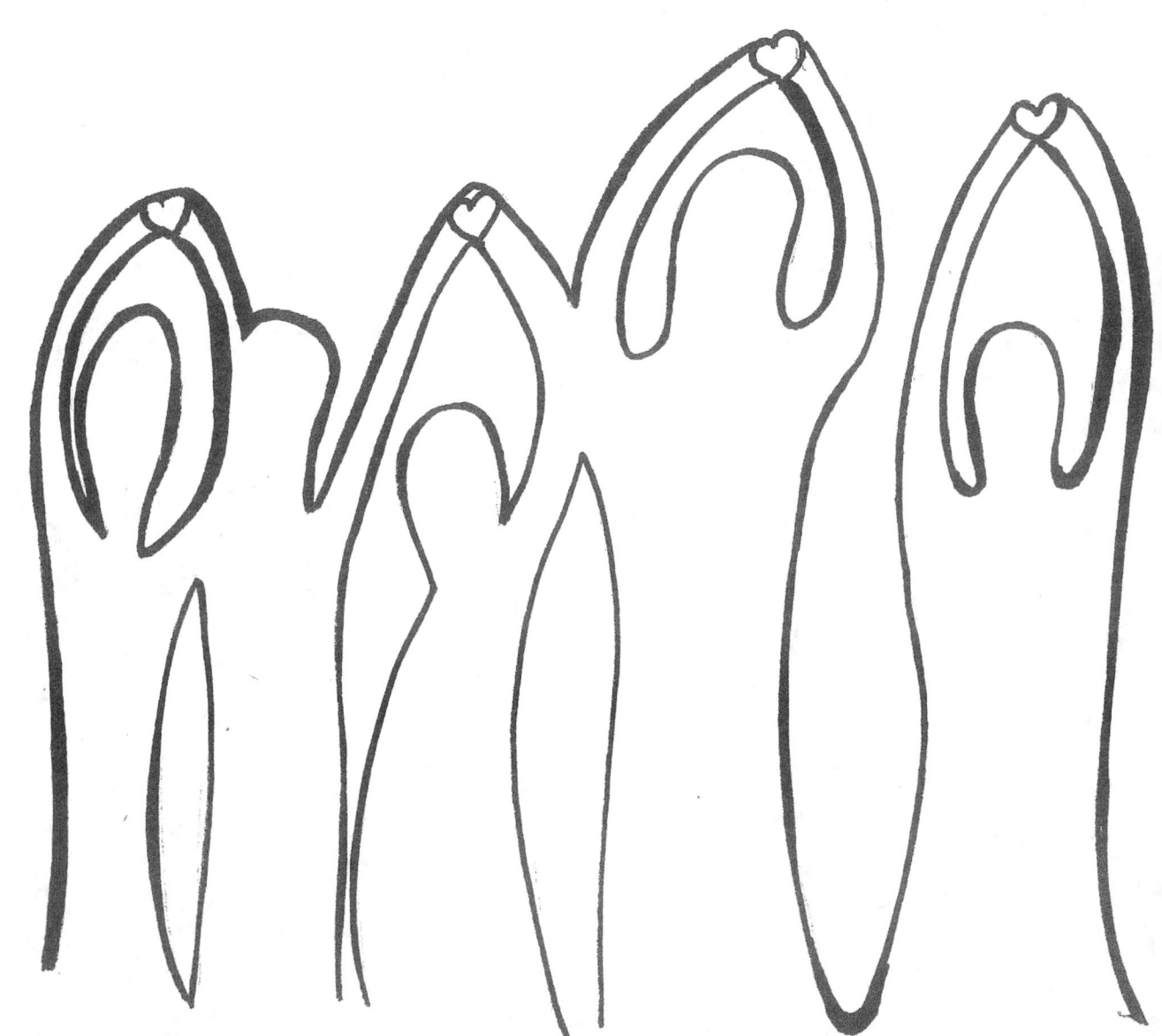

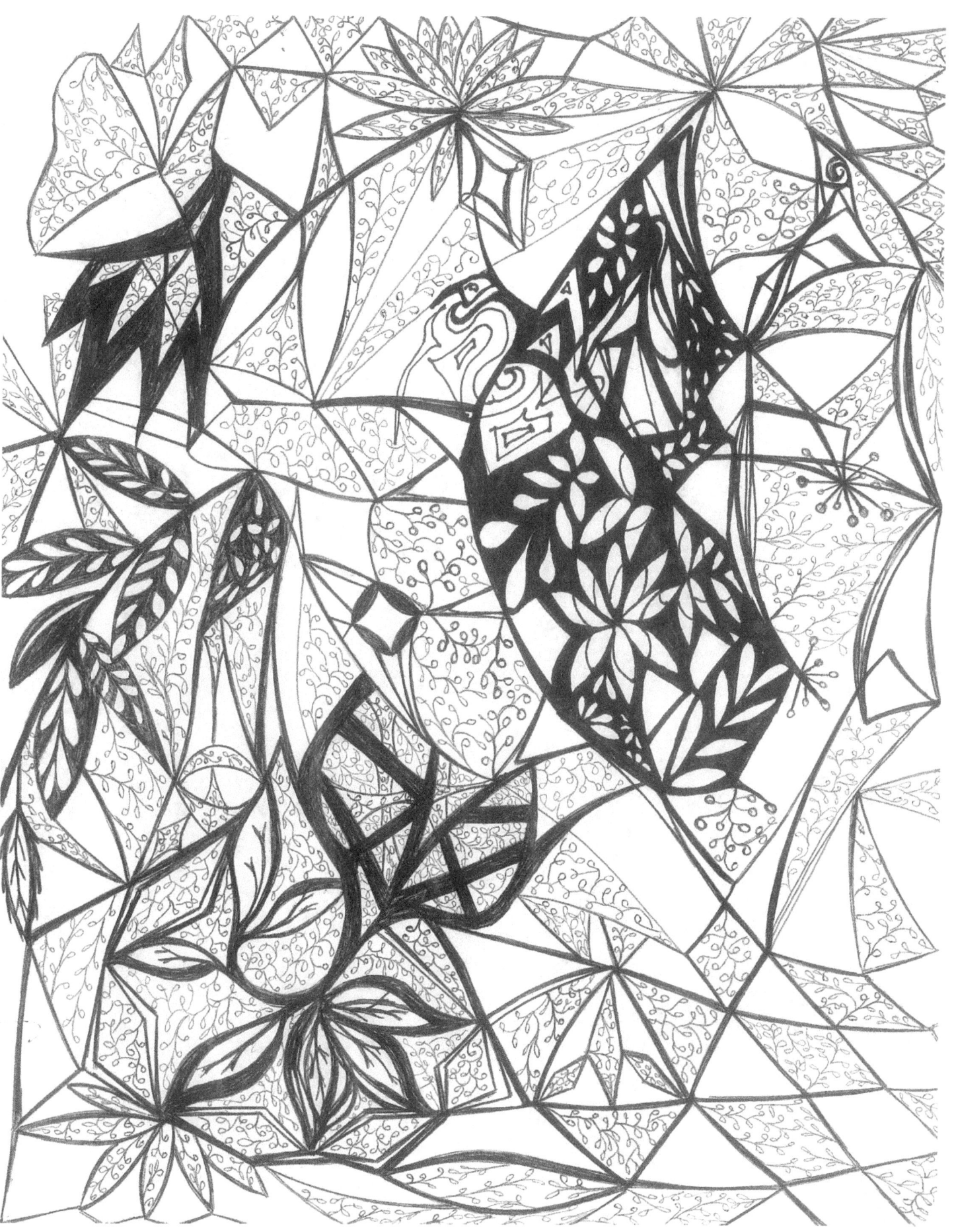

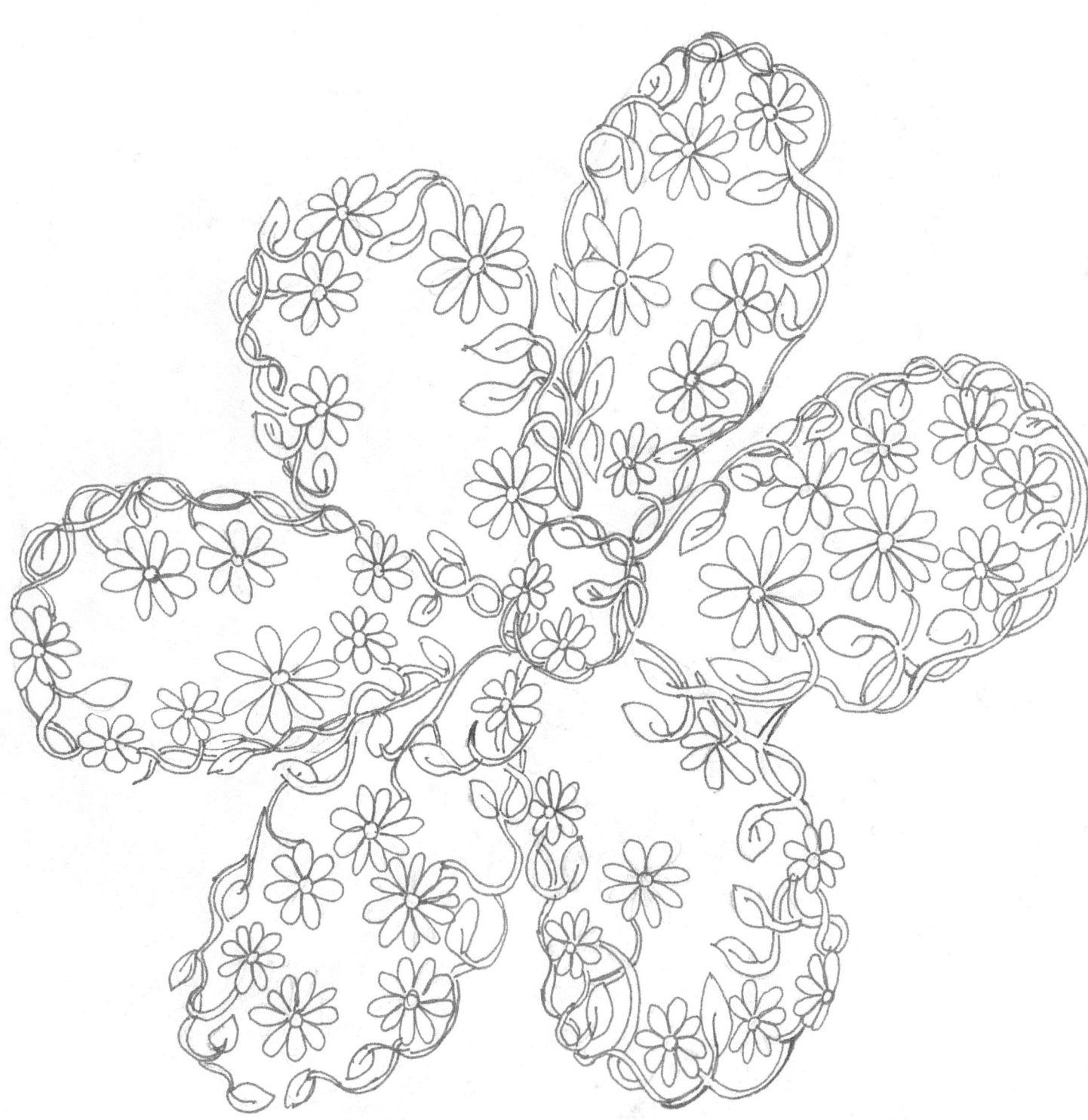

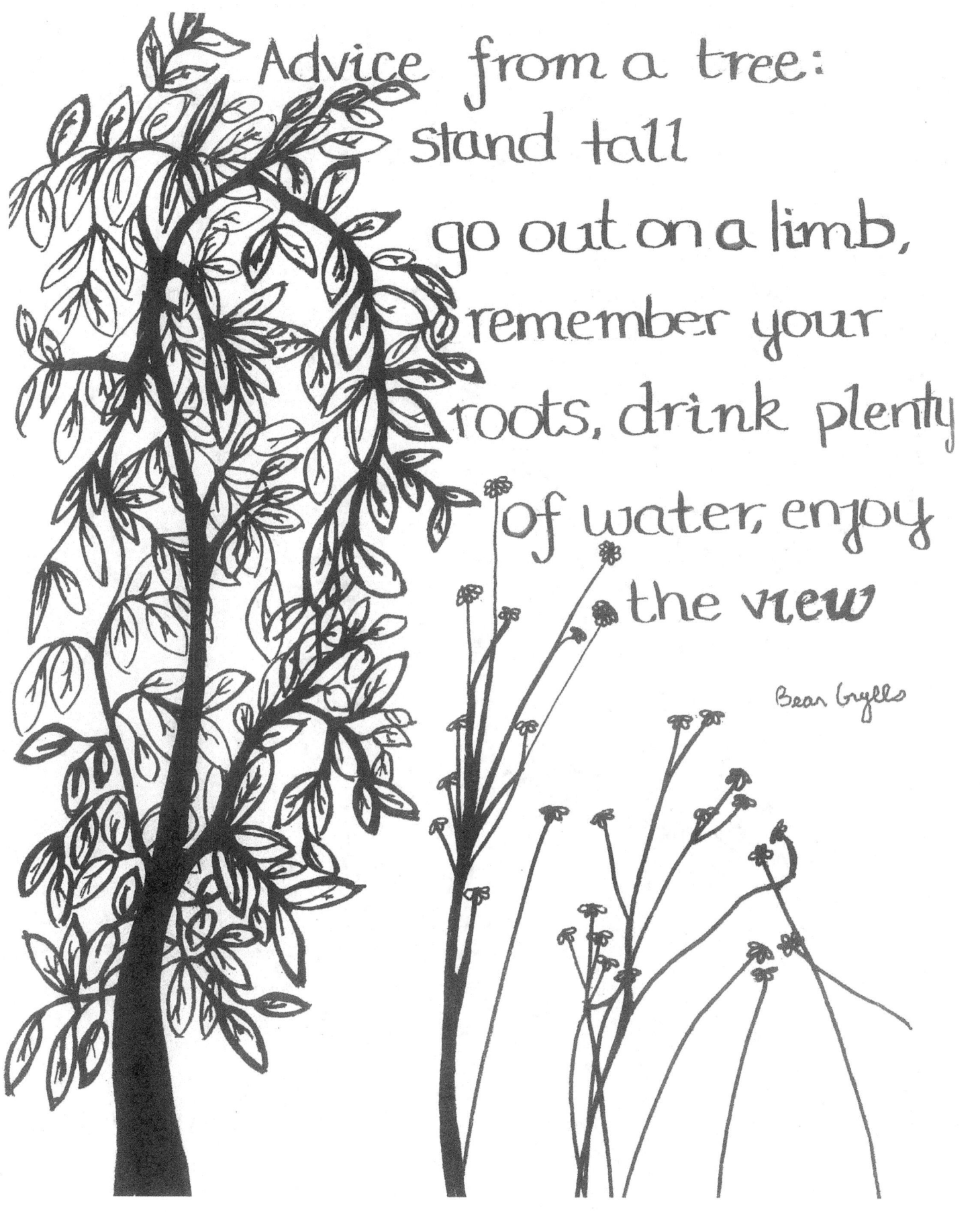

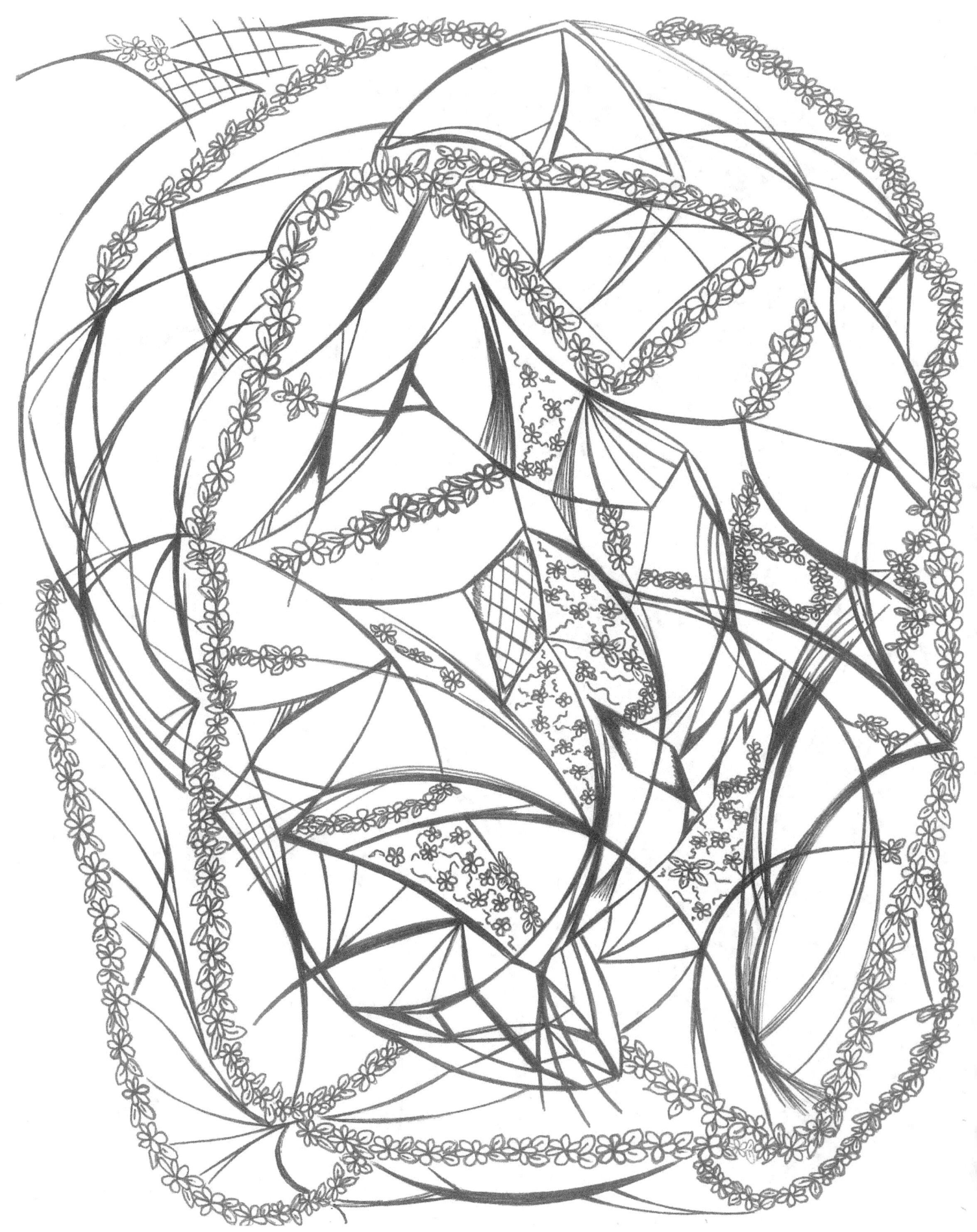

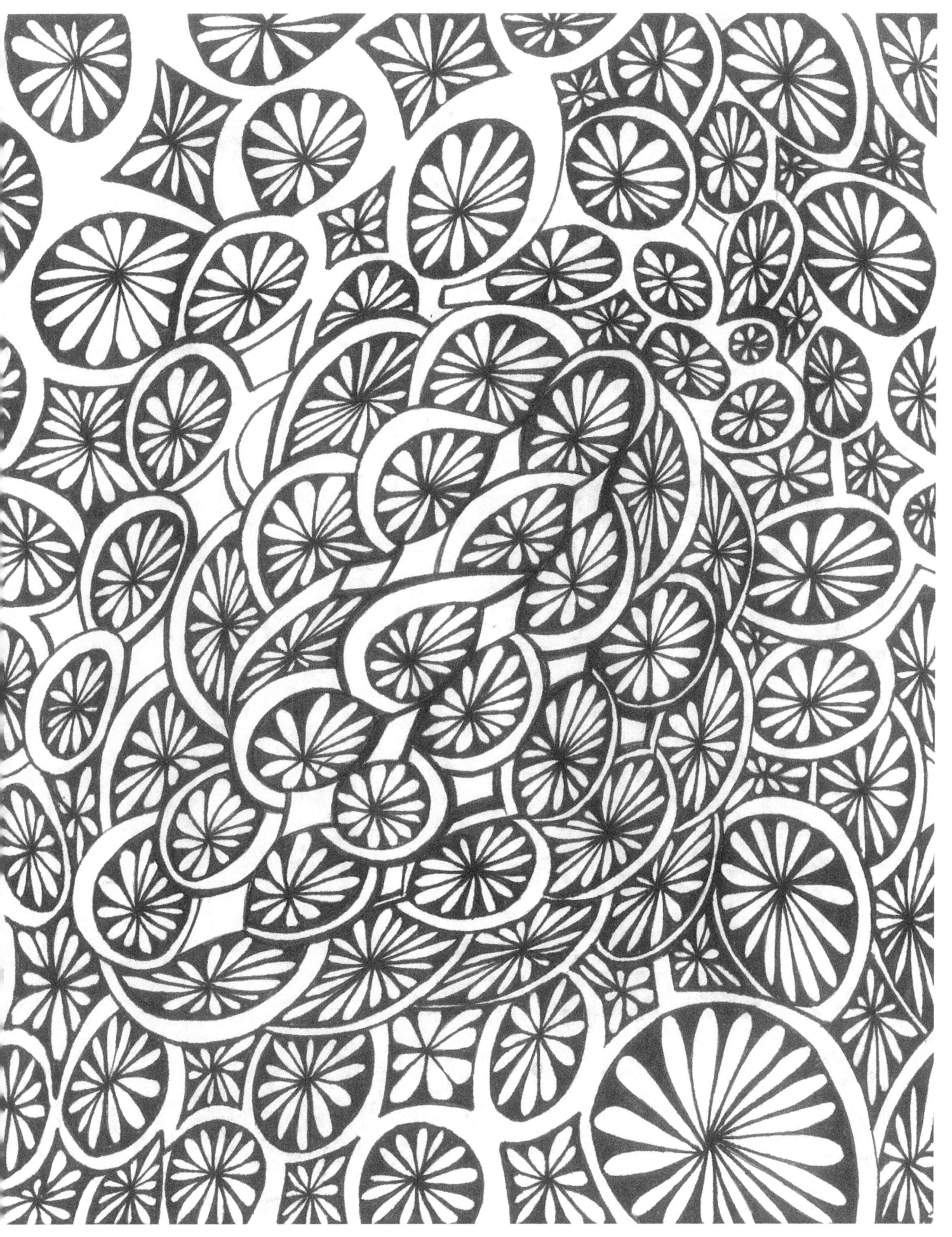

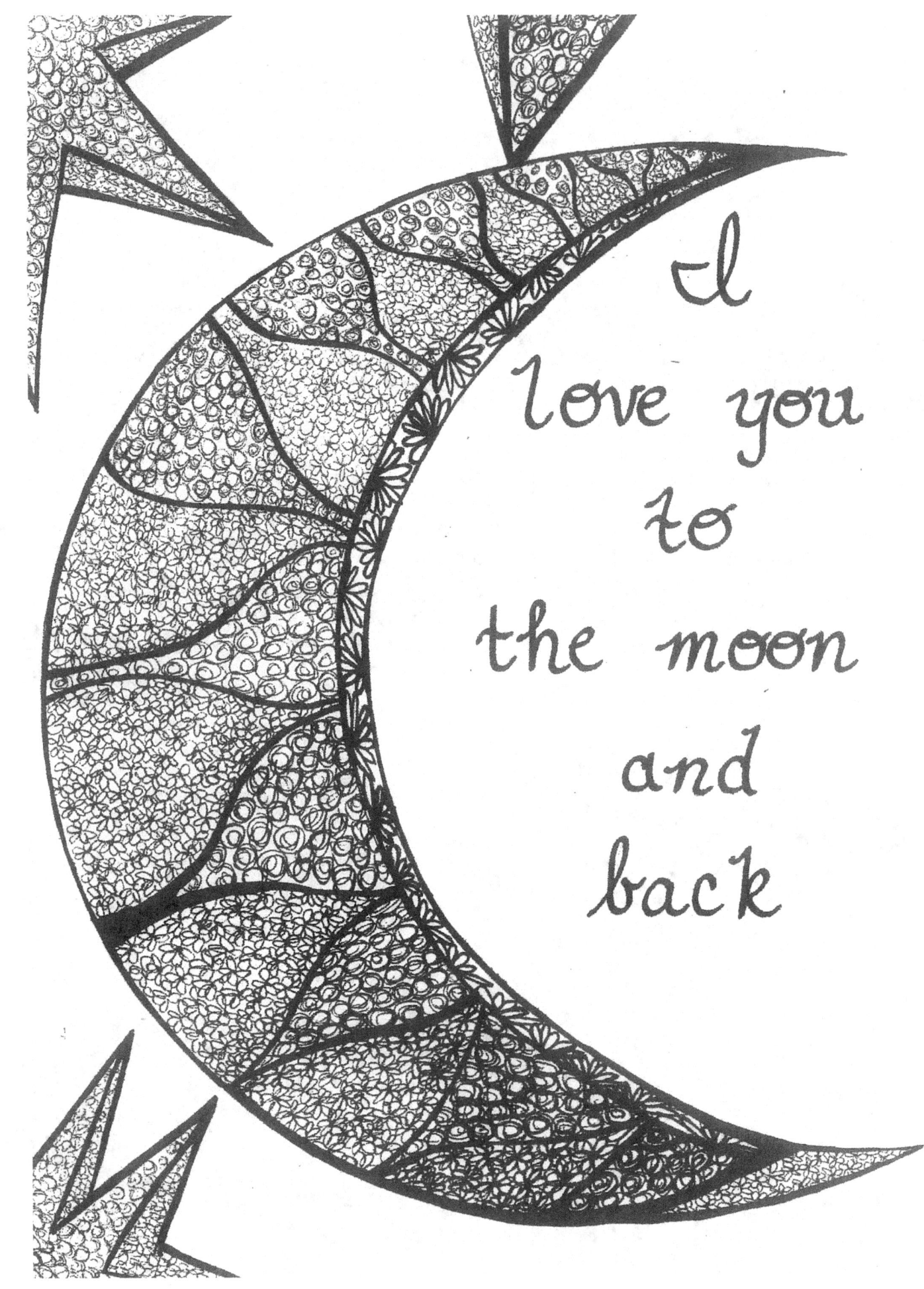

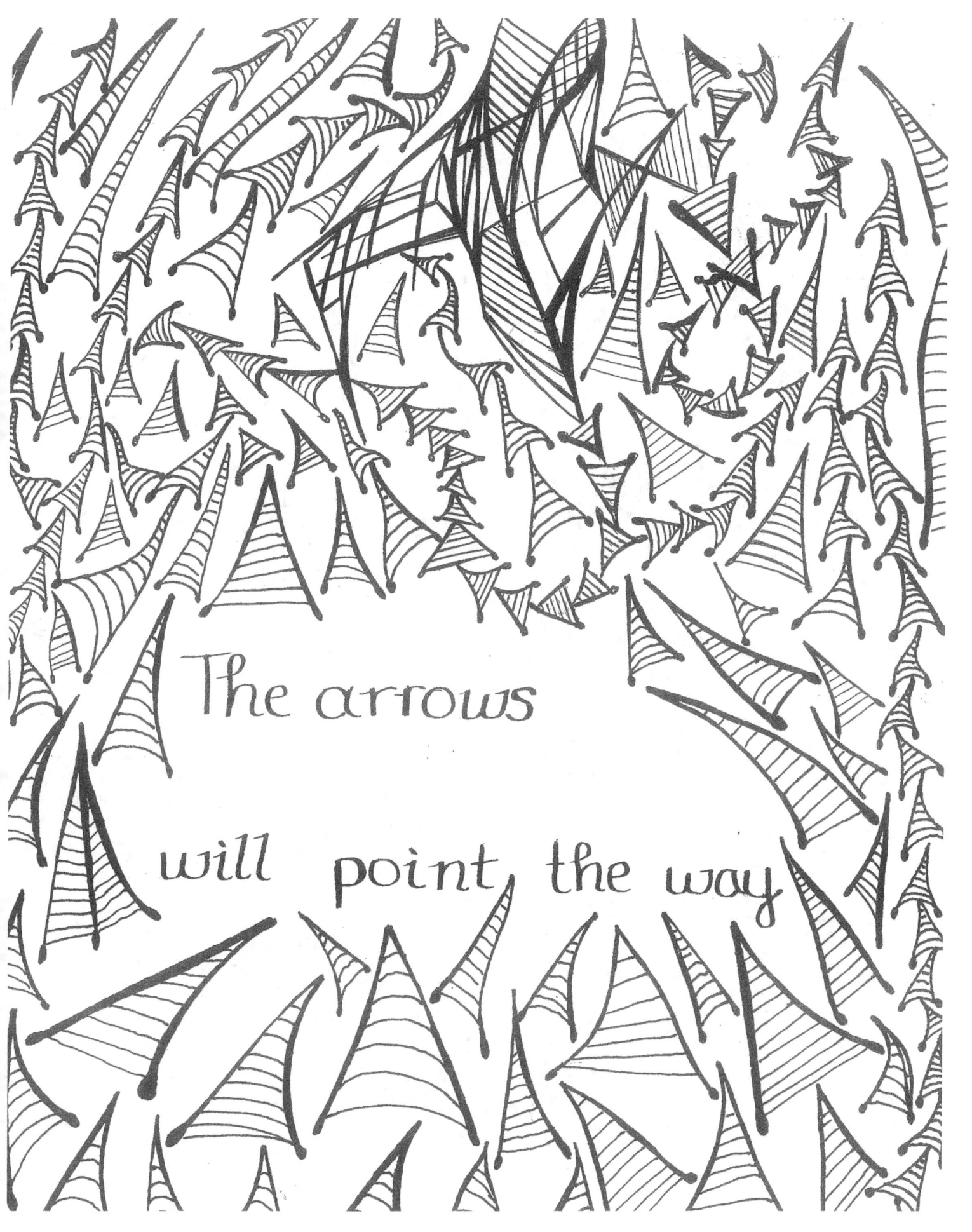

The arrows

will point the way

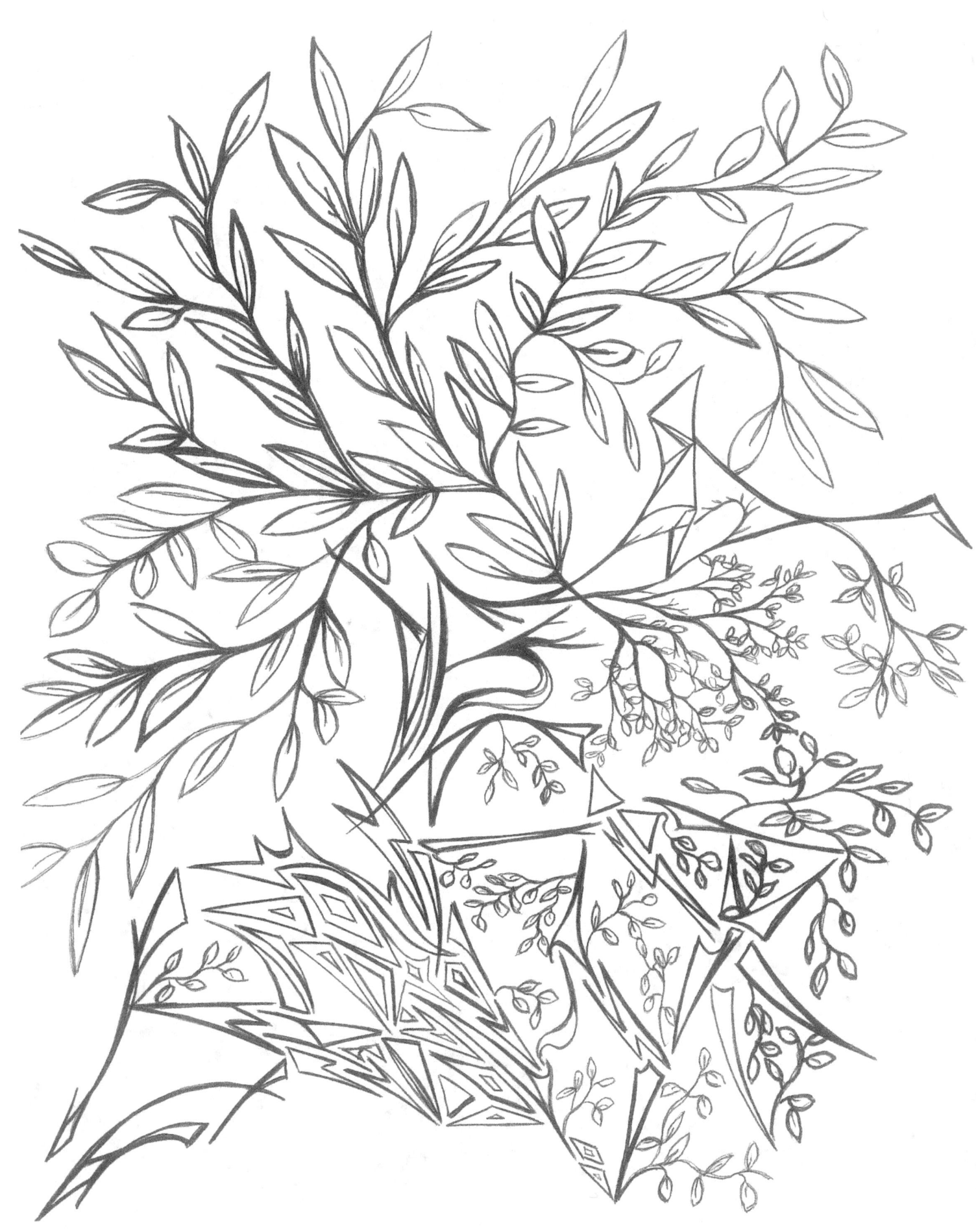

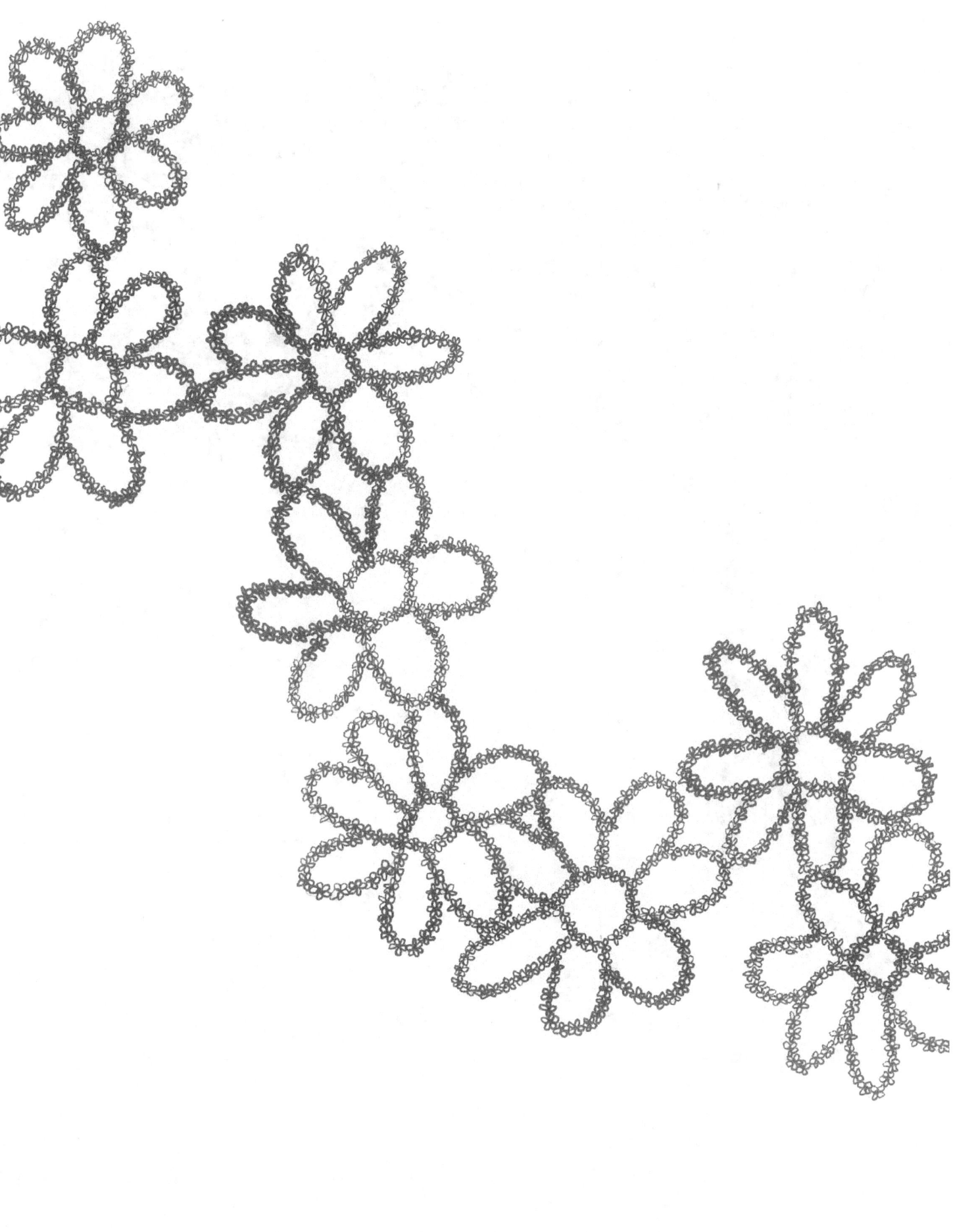

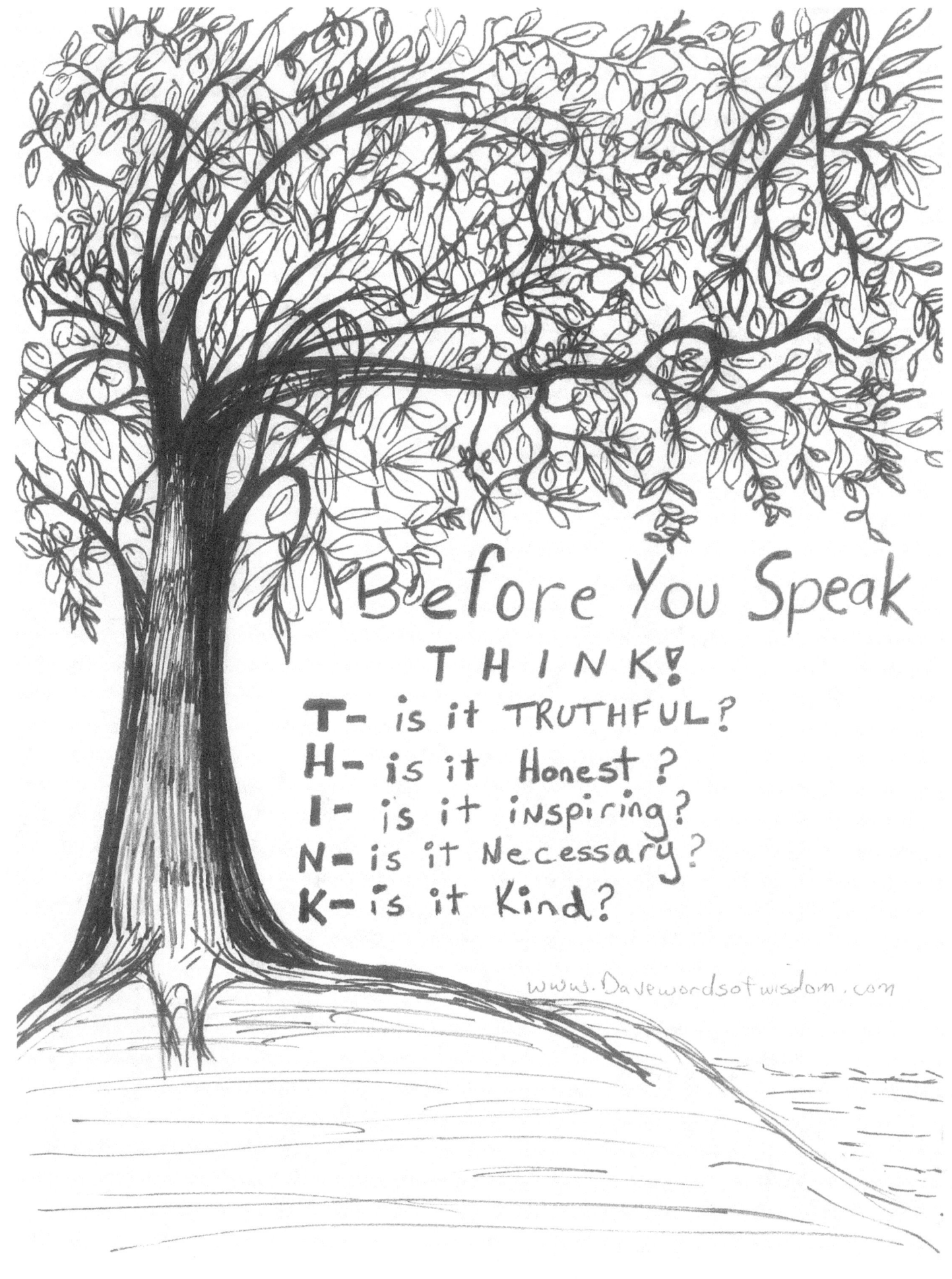

Before You Speak

THINK!

T- is it TRUTHFUL?
H- is it Honest?
I- is it inspiring?
N- is it Necessary?
K- is it Kind?

www.Davewordsofwisdom.com

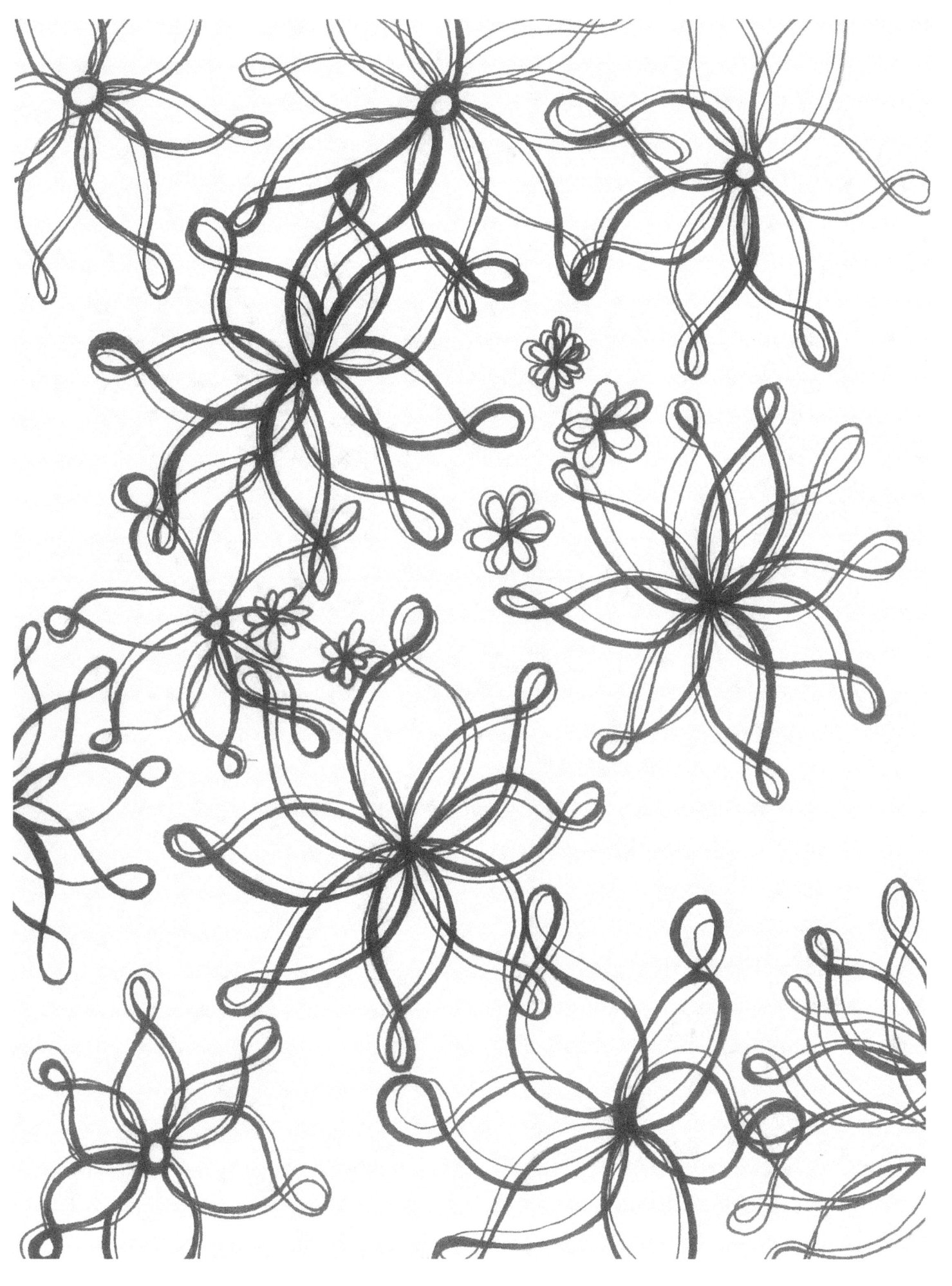

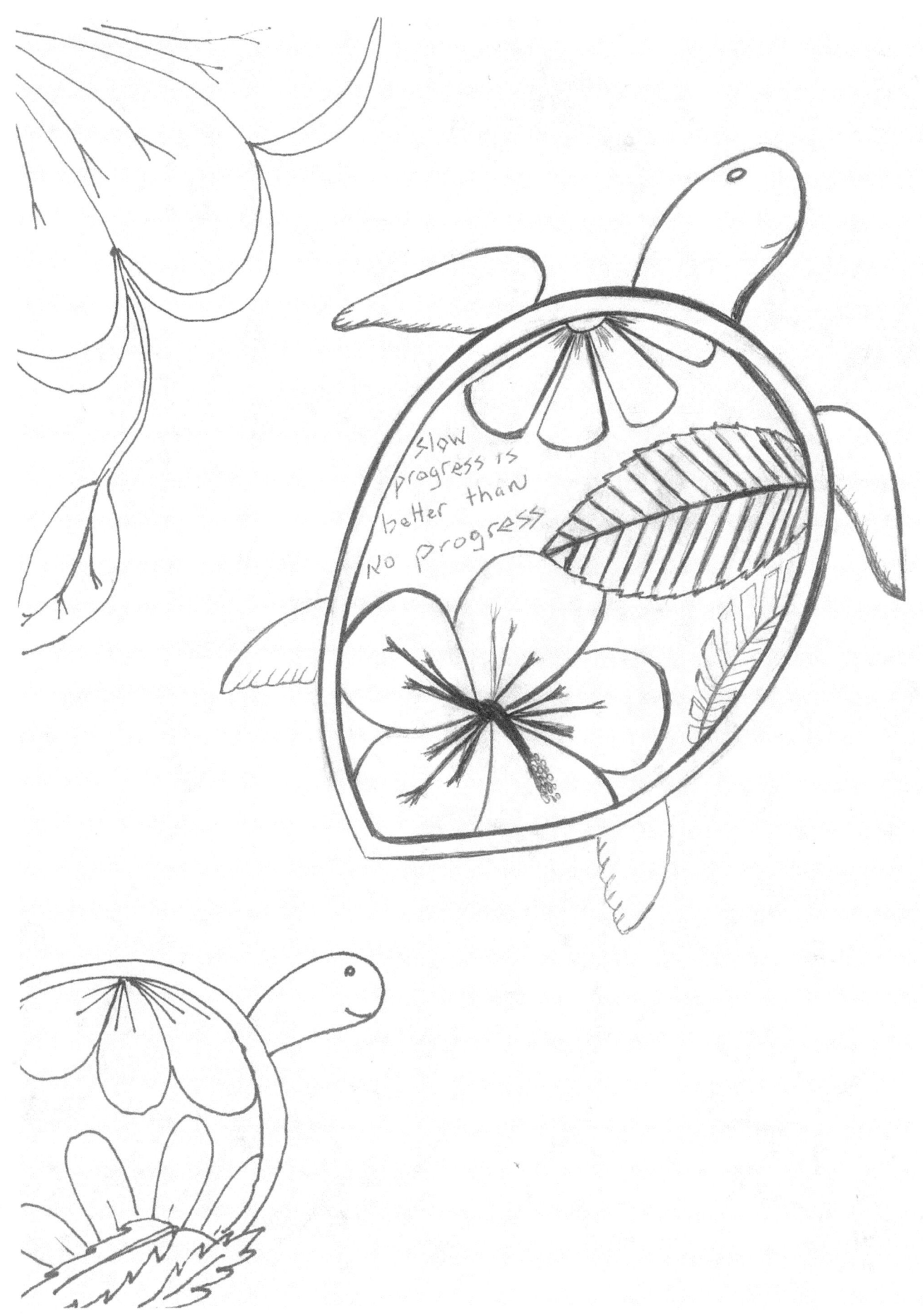

Slow progress is better than No progress

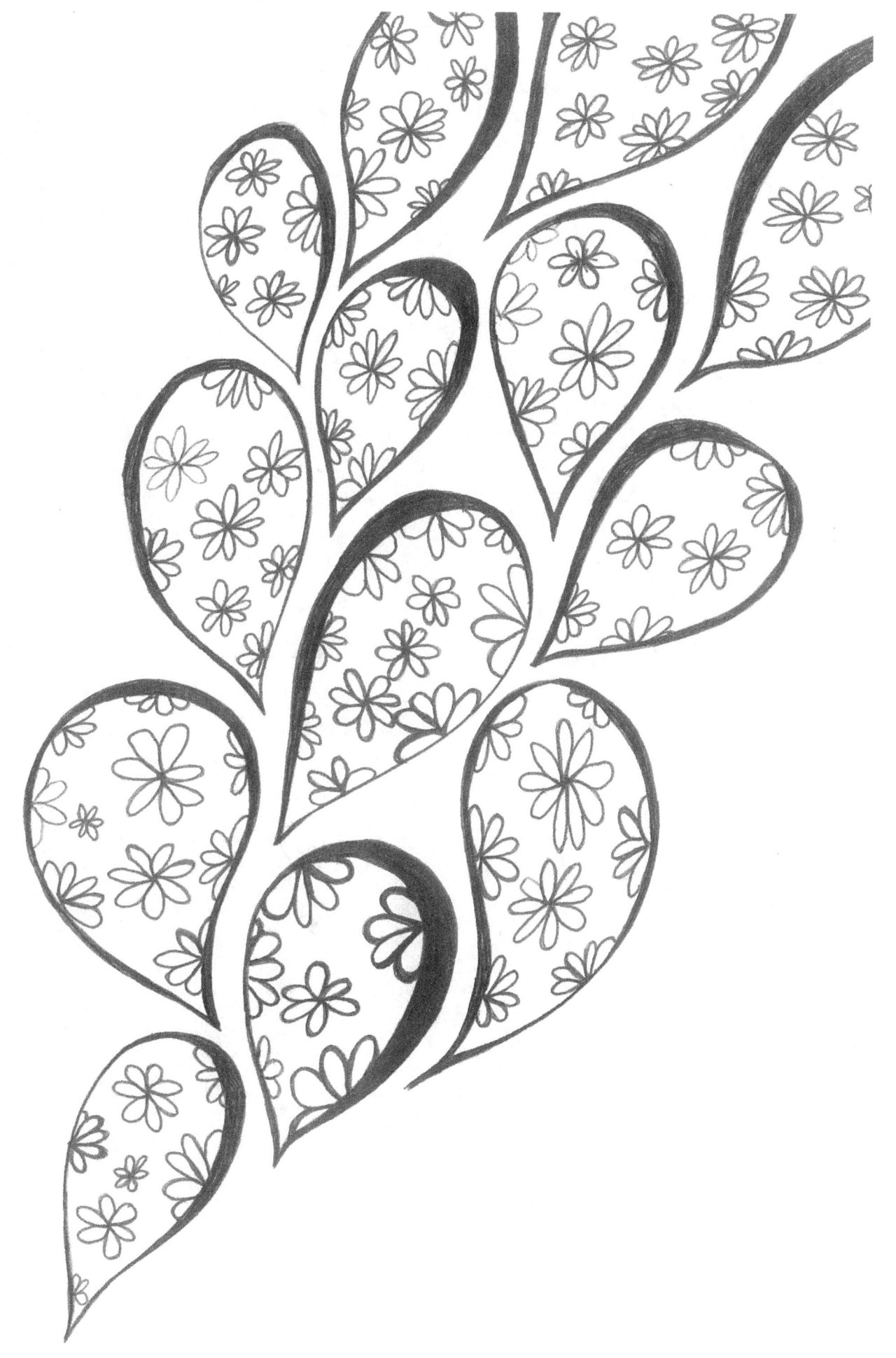

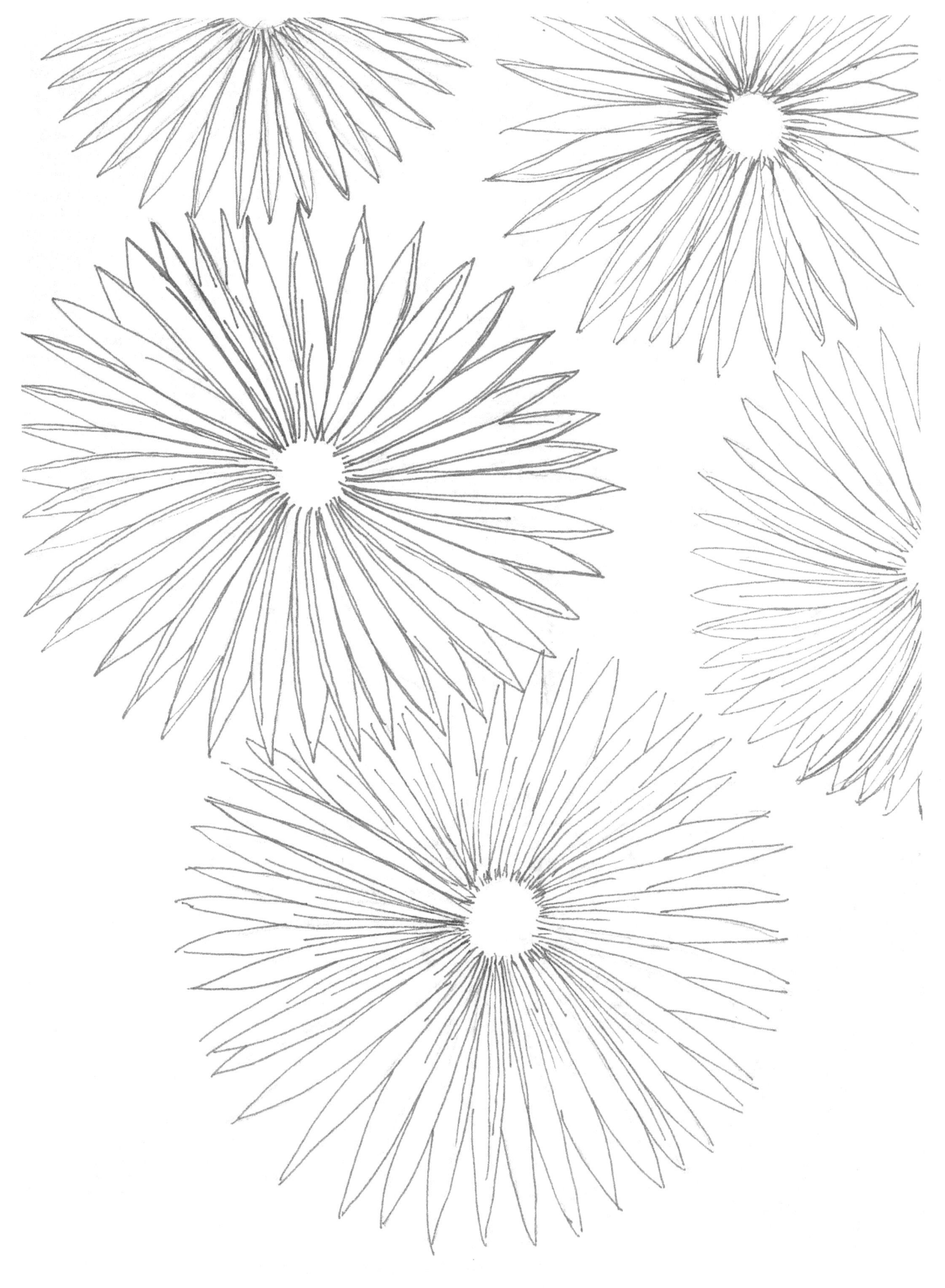

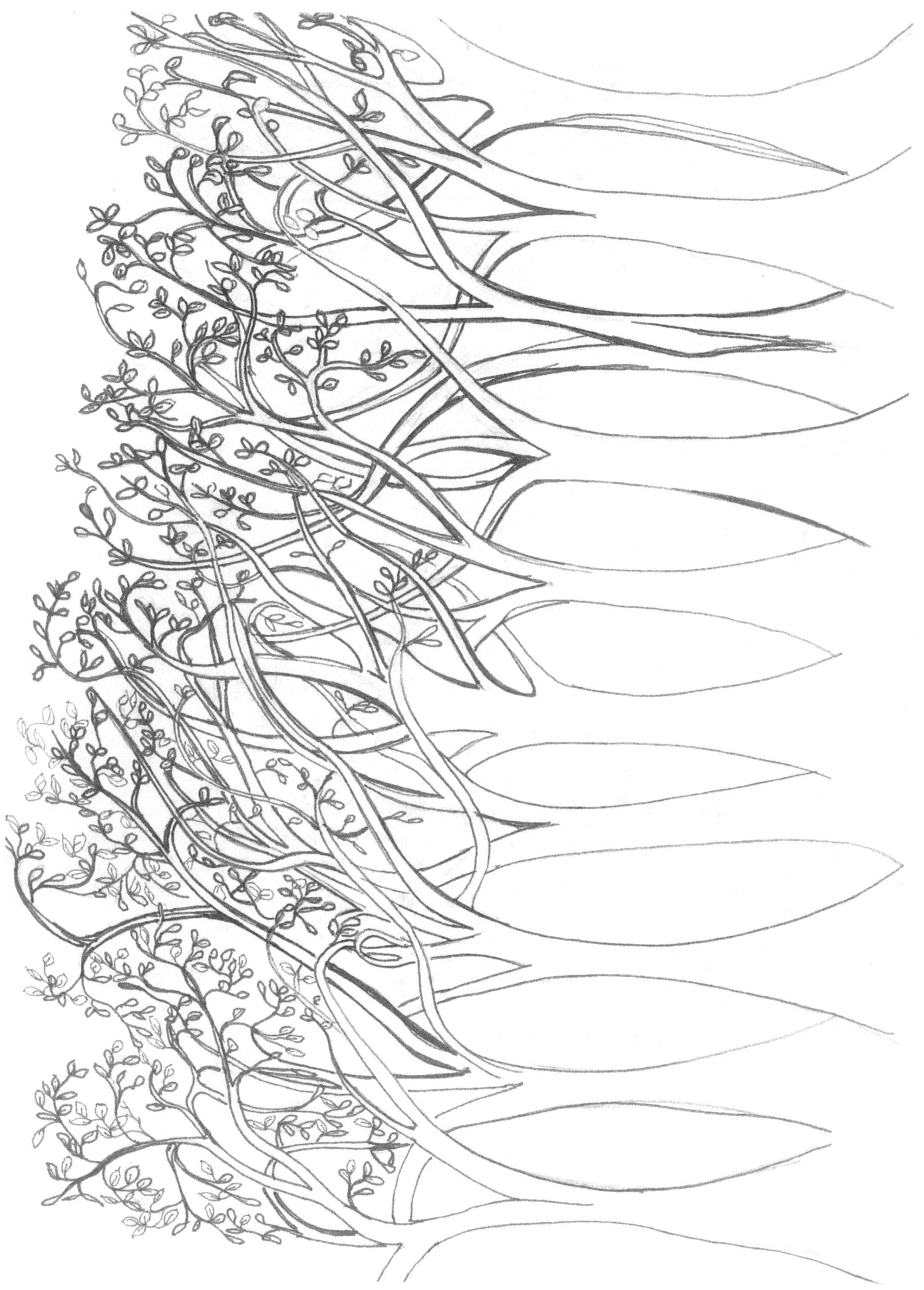

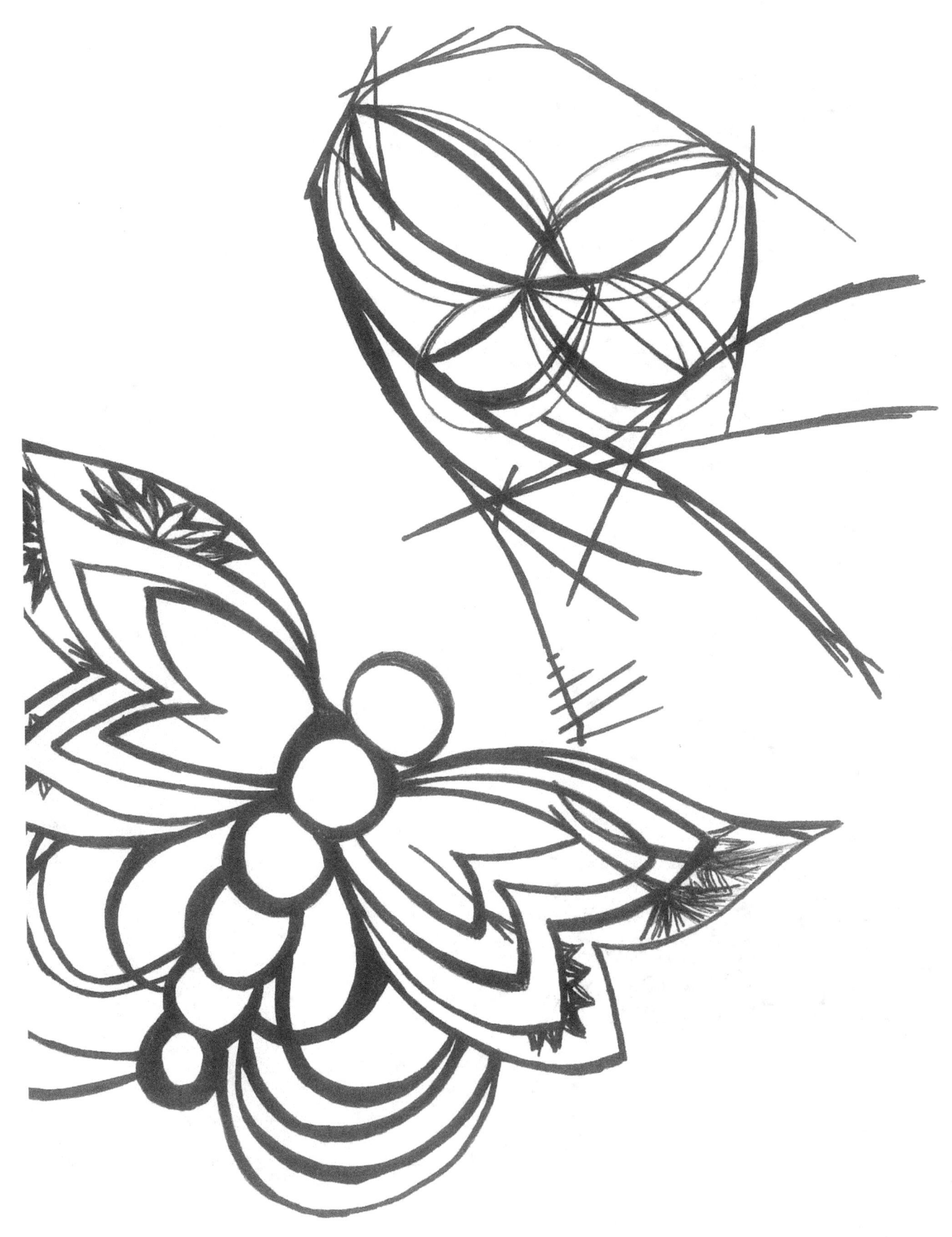

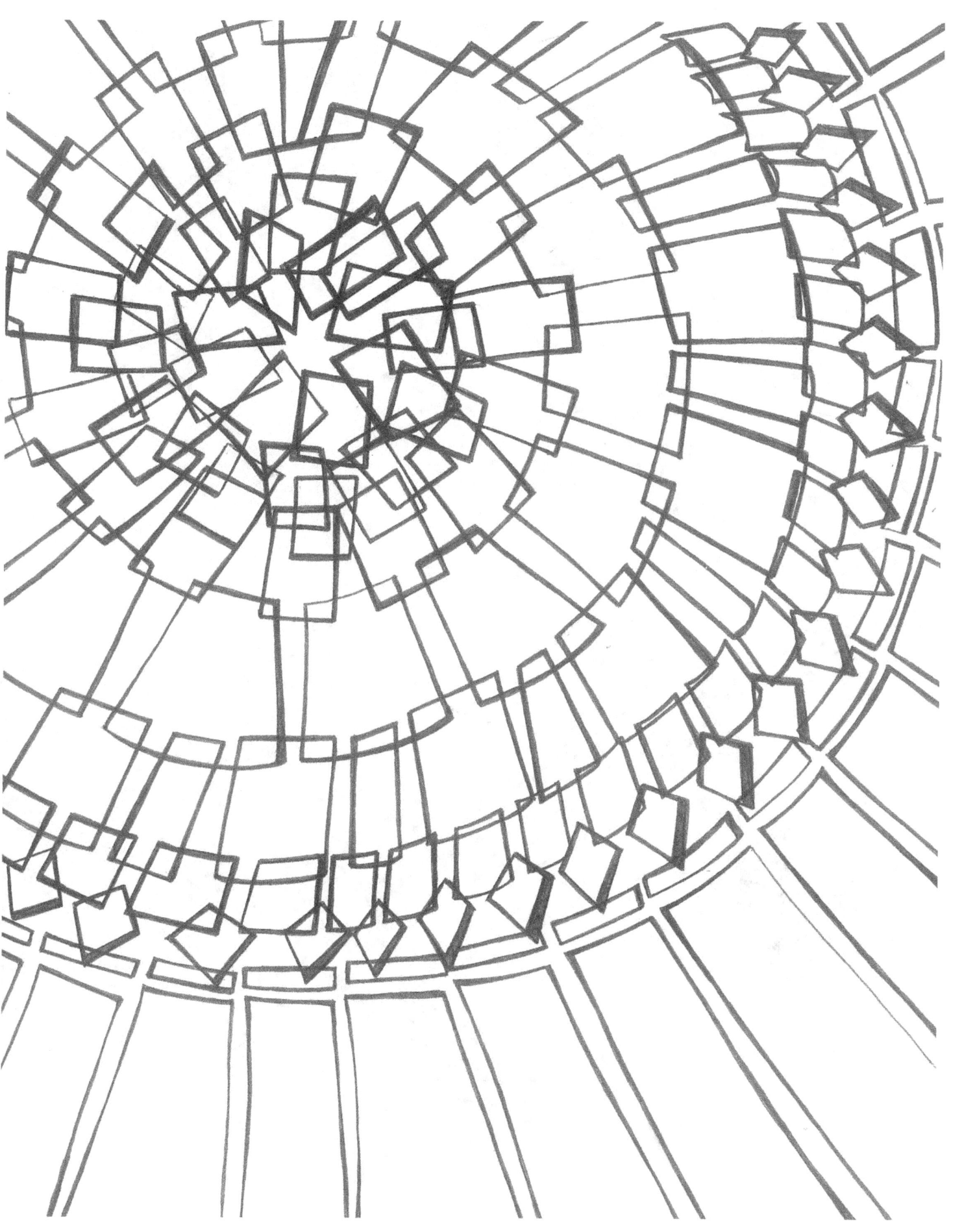

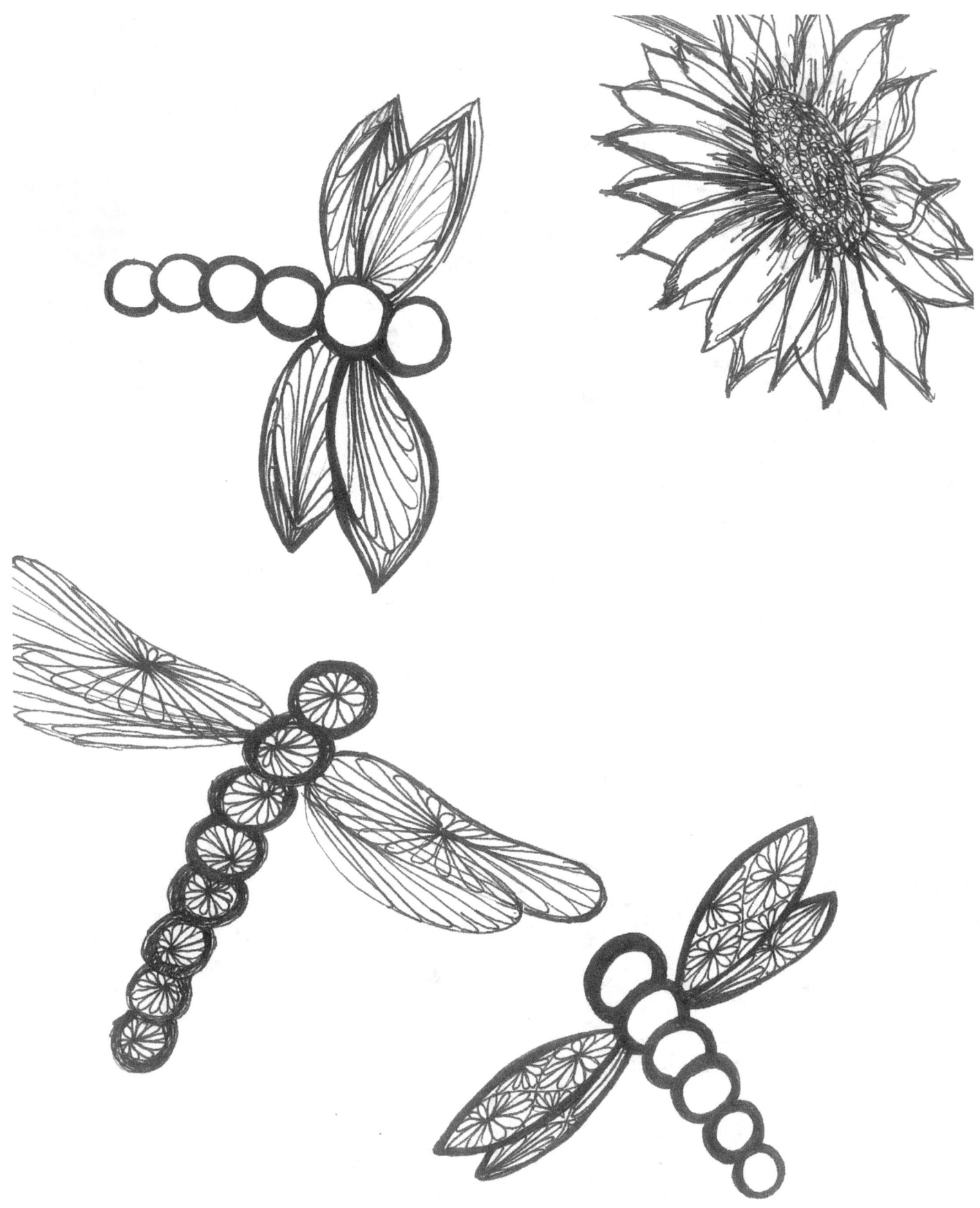

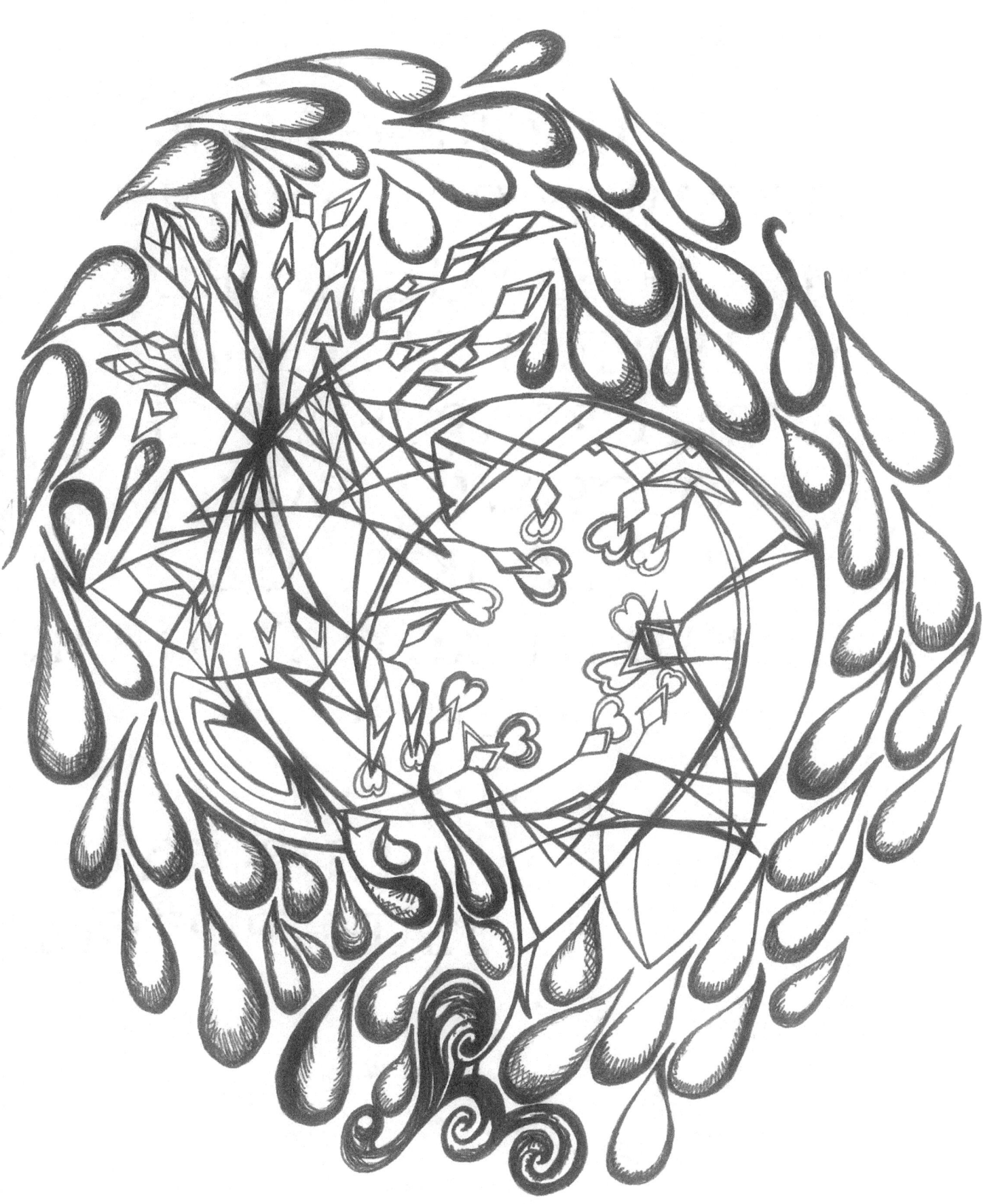

THIS COLORING BOOK
IS MY WAY OF SHOWING
MY GIFT TO THE WORLD.
MY HOPE IS THE PEOPLE
WITH GREAT SENSE OF
COLOR WILL TAKE
THIS BOOK TO ITS
FULL POTENTIAL WITH THEIR
TALENTS.

THANK YOU,
KATIE PIPRUDE